Paris Reflections

PARIS REFLECTIONS

WALKS THROUGH AFRICAN-AMERICAN PARIS

by

Christiann Anderson

and

Monique Y. Wells

The McDonald & Woodward Publishing Company
Blacksburg, Virginia
2002

The McDonald & Woodward Publishing Company
Blacksburg, Virginia

Paris Reflections
Walks through African-American Paris

All rights reserved. First printing March 2002
Printed in the United States of America by
McNaughton & Gunn, Inc., Saline, MI
Distributed by The University of Nebraska Press

10 09 08 07 06 05 04 03 02   10 9 8 7 6 5 4 3 2 1

Library of Congress Cataloging-in-Publication Data

Anderson, Christiann, 1956-
  Paris reflections : walks through African-American Paris / by Christiann
Anderson and Monique Y. Wells.
    p. cm.
Includes bibliographical references and index.
  ISBN 0-939923-88-2 (alk. paper)
  1. Paris (France)--Guidebooks. 2. Walking--France--Paris--Guidebooks.
3. African Americans--Travel--Guidebooks. I. Wells, Monique Y. II. Title.
  DC708 .A58 2002
  914.4'3610484--dc21

                                                          2002002153

Contents

Preface

We, the authors of ***Paris Reflections,*** would like to share with you what the creation of this work means to us.

Christiann Anderson

There is something enchanting to me about holding a well-worn book that has been read many times; I feel as though it is a part of someone's life and not just something to be read. The smell of old books makes me feel comfortable, like being at my grandmother's house, listening to her tell stories, and being transported to another time and place made real through the magic of her words. She presented her history like rare gems that were displayed only for me. During those moments, I was transported into her past; I felt able to walk in her shoes and to see things through her eyes.

When I was young, I loved looking through used book bins

outside bookstores. Those bins provided me with the works of Langston Hughes, James Baldwin, Richard Wright, and others, and I discovered that many African Americans had left the United States to make France their home. This intrigued me; I wanted to know more about each person and what made France special to them. As I read more and more books by and about African-American writers, painters, scientists, entertainers, and designers who lived and created in Paris, I knew that Paris was where I wanted to be.

My first trip to the City of Light was a short two-week holiday with a tour group. Being here was like walking through a painting where I could touch things as I went along. Window displays looked like theater sets, pastries crossed over from the realm of "make believe" into heavenly gastronomic reality, and the beauty of the city at night left me breathless. My second trip to Paris has lasted ten years, and I am still counting!

Paris Reflections: Walks through African-American Paris presents an opportunity to walk through the streets where a unique chapter in African-American history was made abroad . . . . to walk in the footsteps of those whose contributions to France were so significant that their magic still captivates and endures . . . . to see the City of Light anew, inspired by the fact that many African Americans have lived here before, and that many still do.

For me, walking through Paris is a daily celebration in honor of Josephine Baker, James Baldwin, Langston Hughes, and the many, many others whose dreams have come true in this beautiful city. It is my sincere hope that this book will become that magical, well-worn edition that becomes a companion for your walks through Paris. And perhaps you too will feel that it is possible to walk through our history here, touching things as you go along, and seeing this old, beautiful city with a unique African-American perspective.

Monique Y. Wells

For me, **Paris Reflections** represents a unique opportunity to share some of the adventures and achievements that African Americans have experienced in Paris. I have loved Paris since the first day that I moved here in 1992, and have been on a quest to uncover its many mysteries since that time.

I was inspired to come to Paris because of my love of the French language and my desire to perfect my use of it. Upon arrival, my passion for things culinary quickly manifested itself, and I devoted myself to searching for the flakiest *croissants,* the best *magret de canard,* and the finest *tarte tatin* that the city could offer. I also took the time to visit the major monuments and museums such as Notre-Dame and the Louvre, but my interest in their history was minimal. I have since learned that African Americans have significantly contributed to the history of Paris, and indeed of France, and that events significant to us took place at these sites. I now look at these monuments with a fresh perspective.

I slowly became aware that African Americans had settled and flourished in their chosen professions in Paris. Barbara Chase-Riboud and Jessye Norman spring to mind as contemporary examples. I read Reginald Lewis' autobiography and realized that his orchestration of the takeover of a French conglomerate was brought to fruition on the same square that had seen the guillotine take the lives of over 1000 French people during the French revolution about 200 years before. I was aware of the legend of Josephine Baker as a performer, but was stunned to learn that she had participated in the French Resistance effort during World War II and was given a state funeral in Paris. I gradually awakened to the fact that many, many African Americans had come here before me – and that African-American and French history were intertwined. And I wanted to know more.

I began to see the streets of Paris in a new light. I read and read and walked the streets again. And I began to see traces of the presence of black people in Paris – a painting of a black man serving a hot beverage to a white woman on the facade of a building, a plaque dedicated to Richard Wright on an apartment building, a statue honoring Alexandre Dumas. . . . It became evident that I had only scratched the surface of what promised to be a treasure trove of history. I continue to investigate the events of our past in Paris, and also to chronicle current events involving African Americans here.

From my research, I created a series of self-guided walks on African-American history in Paris for my travel business, Discover Paris! These are the inspiration for *Paris Reflections*. I hope that the information contained within the pages of this book will inspire African Americans to venture to Paris and see firsthand the places where our achievements have been realized, respected, and celebrated when we could not hope for similar recognition at home.

Monique Y. Wells

Introduction

Many famous and not-so-famous African Americans have spent a portion of their lives in Paris as visitors or residents – working, studying, finding themselves and their place as Black people in the world. Among them are writers, painters, architects, scientists, attorneys, musicians, and other performers. In the 1800s, for example, there were Victor Séjour (playwright) and Ira Aldridge (actor), both quite successful in their respective fields. Séjour was a Paris resident for twenty-eight years, and his work was extremely popular during his lifetime. He died in Paris in 1874 and was buried in Père Lachaise cemetery. William Wells Brown, an escaped slave and prolific writer, spent a great deal of time in Paris before the Civil War. He wrote very fondly of Paris in his publication *Sketches of Places and People Abroad* (1855).

In the early twentieth century, World War I was the critical event that caused French and African-American history to become irrevocably entwined. African-American troops entered the fighting under French command, and found themselves not only accepted for who they were and what they accomplished, but also publicly recognized for it. White American soldiers, and particularly officers, were both astonished and dismayed at the manner in which the French embraced black American troops. The experience was one that the soldiers never forgot. And once the war was over, many returned to France, the country where one could simply "be himself" and not face the daily trials and tribulations of living in a bigoted and institutionally unequal society.

The "crazy years" after World War I saw jazz enter the scene and rapidly become king of the music world. It was the African-American musicians present in Paris after World War I who were responsible for introducing jazz to the French and making it the most popular form of music to sweep the capital. Between this new "hot" music and the amazing catapult to stardom experienced by Josephine Baker in the show *La Revue Nègre*, Paris was swept up into what was locally called *négrophilie*, a fascination with black culture. Practically everyone is aware of Baker, who adopted France as her second home and developed a remarkable career spanning fifty years in Paris beginning in 1925. In this same era, African-American writers and artists from the Harlem Renaissance also lived and worked here – Langston Hughes, Jessie Fauset, Palmer Hayden, and Augusta Savage figure among them.

Montmartre, or "MoMart" as it was affectionately called by blacks of the era, became the center of the first African-American community in Paris during the interwar years. Black Americans opened restaurants, nightclubs, and other businesses in this area. Langston Hughes got his first job in Paris in one of these clubs, the then-famous Le Grand Duc. Josephine Baker, Bricktop, and Palmer and Florence Jones were among the performers who lit up the nights in the shadow of Sacré-Cœur Basilica. The African-American artists in Paris during this time tended to settle on the Left Bank, but the majority of the activity in the black American community centered on Montmartre. Nightclubs were very successful, and Bricktop's club in particular became so well known that she began to attract a very wealthy white European and American clientele.

The stock market crash of 1929 forced many white Americans in Paris to leave Europe, as they no longer had the tremendous buying power that they had enjoyed during the "crazy years." But it was the advent of World War II that caused this small but thriving community to dismantle. The Nazi invasion of 1940 sealed its fate – Americans of all races risked detainment in prison camps if they did not leave the country.

African-American Eugene Bullard, a World War I pilot who fought with the French and was decorated by the French military, chose to stay in Paris after the occupation. Since WWI he had managed or owned several nightclubs and other businesses in Montmartre, including Le Grand Duc. He wanted to aid his adopted country once again in war, but was wounded and forced to flee the French capital on foot as the Nazis pressed their offensive southward. Pianist Arthur Briggs was another of the few who refused to leave; he was interned in a camp north of Paris for several years. Josephine Baker joined the French armed forces as an auxiliary to the French Air Force, and also participated in covert activities for the French Resistance movement. She was never discovered or captured.

After World War II, many black soldiers took advantage of the GI Bill to come to Paris to study. Subjects ranged from visual arts at the Ecole des Beaux-Arts to philosophy at the Sorbonne. African Americans operated businesses, opened restaurants, and lived here in relative peace and tranquility compared to the environment of racist hostility and repression in the United States. A substantial African-American community was thus established, and was highlighted by the presence of some of the finest writers of the period. The most famous of these were Richard Wright and James Baldwin, both of whom spent several years in Paris and died on French soil.

The 1960s brought political upheaval to many countries around the world, and France was no exception. The French had been embroiled in a nasty war with Algeria for several years, and African Americans saw the increasingly tattered myth of a "color-blind" France that had enticed so many to come to Paris after WWI utterly destroyed as they observed Arabs being beaten in the streets. The resulting French student uprising of 1968 led to a virtual shutdown of the country, and a few African Americans assisted the students in their standoff against the government. Once order was restored, the French police force became much more aggressive about checking the identity papers of *all* people of color. It became evident that France wasn't that different from America after all. Many African

Americans who resided in Paris during this time wrestled with the question of whether or not they should go back home to participate in the struggle for civil rights or stay in a country which had clearly dispelled any illusions of being a haven from racism.

Today, over forty years after the beginning of the civil rights movement in America, a significant number of African Americans still call Paris home. And interestingly, many find that their nationality plays more of a role in their acceptance in society than does their race. More and more business and professional people have taken their place in the African-American community beside those in the arts; attorneys, journalists, and engineers are among the Black professionals currently residing here. Thus the community in Paris is as diverse as any to be found in the United States.

African Americans have a rich and significant history in Paris of which we can be proud. As African Americans, the authors of *Paris Reflections* hope that knowledge of this history will enhance your desire to visit Paris and help you appreciate the city once you arrive.

The walks outlined in *Paris Reflections* provide you with the opportunity to visit six different areas of Paris that are important to African-American history, culture, and contemporary life. A list of calendar dates relevant to African-American history in Paris and quotations from prominent African Americans who have visited (and loved) the city provide further insight into African-American history in Paris.

Additionally, *Paris Reflections* contains a section of travel tips and special pages for jotting down your daily activities and personal impressions during your visit. In the travel tips section you will find invaluable practical information that covers the layout of the city, modes of transportation, resources available in English, information on telephoning, changing money, and a host of other things that you will need to know for your journey. Even travelers who have visited Paris before may find information in this section that was previously unknown to them.

We hope that *Paris Reflections: Walks Through African-American Paris* will serve both as inspiration and as a useful tool for your trip. *Bon voyage!*

SIGNIFICANT DATES FOR AFRICAN-AMERICAN HISTORY IN PARIS

JANUARY

January 1 – Patrick Kelly died of AIDS in Paris in 1990.

January 17 – Richard Wright's daughter Rachel was born at the American Hospital in Paris (Neuilly-sur-Seine) in 1949.

January 30-31 – Toni Morrison and James Baldwin were featured at a conference on the American novel, sponsored by New York University and held at the Modern Art Museum of Paris (16th *arrondissement*) in 1982.

FEBRUARY

February 5-9 – A conference on "African Americans and Europe" was held at the Sorbonne (5th *arrondissement*). This was the occasion for the dedication of a plaque from the French government in honor of Richard Wright in 1992.

February 16 – A revival of George Gershwin's *Porgy and Bess*, starring Leontyne Price and Maya Angelou, opened at the Salle Wagram (17th *arrondissement*) in 1953. The opera ran for several months due to its great success.

February 19-21 – The Pan-African Congress, organized by W. E. B. Du Bois, was held at the Grand Hôtel (9th *arrondissement*) next to place de l'Opéra in 1919.

MARCH

March 4 – Bantam-weight boxing champion "Panama" Al Brown regained his title by defeating Sangchili at the Palais des Sports (15th *arrondissement*) in 1938.

March 13 – A benefit concert was held at the Salle Wagram (17th *arrondissement*) on behalf of jazz pianist Bud Powell, who was hospitalized with tuberculosis and needed help with his medical bills in 1964.

March 23 – At the age of 66, Anna Julia Cooper was the first African American to obtain a doctoral degree from the Sorbonne (5th *arrondissement*) in 1925.

APRIL

April 15 – Josephine Baker was honored with a state funeral in Paris after her death on April 10, 1975. An estimated 20,000 people crowded around La Madeleine (8th *arrondissement*), the church in which the ceremony was held, to bid her farewell.

April 21 – Lorraine Hansbury's play *A Raisin in the Sun* opened at the Théâtre de la Porte Saint-Martin (10th *arrondissement*) in 1979.

April 24-27 – A conference on "African-American Music and Europe" was held at the Sorbonne (5th *arrondissement*). The jazz master Sidney Bechet was honored on April 25, 1996.

ANNIVERSARY DATES . . . . CONTINUED

MAY

May 13 – Vertamae Grosvenor and Julia Wright assisted French students in their 1968 revolt against the administration of the Sorbonne (5th *arrondissement*) and later, the police.

May 14 – Sidney Bechet, who became a legendary figure in the Paris jazz world, died in the Paris suburb of Garches on his 62nd birthday in 1959.

May 16 – Angela Davis was invited to appear on French television station Antenne 2 (8th *arrondissement*) in a panel discussion on racism in 1975.

JUNE

June 15 – Bessie Coleman received her international pilot's license from the International Aeronautical Federation (16th *arrondissement*) in 1921.

June 18 – The first Juneteenth celebration in Paris was held at Haynes' Restaurant (Paris's oldest soul food restaurant – 9th *arrondissement*) in 1994. The event was sponsored by SISTERS – An Association of Black-American Women in France.

June 27 – Boxer Jack Johnson defeated the "great white hope" Francis Moran at the Cirque d'Hiver (11th *arrondissement*) in 1914.

JULY

July 14 – Opera singer Jessye Norman presided over the Bastille Day ceremony honoring the 200th anniversary of the French Revolution (8th *arrondissement*) in 1989.

July 15 – Sally Hemings, the slave and mistress of Thomas Jefferson, arrived in Paris in 1787 at the age of 15. Their affair reportedly began in Paris in a residence on the corner of rue de Berri and the Champs-Elysées (8th *arrondissement*).

July 19 – Langston Hughes addressed the International Writers' Congress at the Théâtre de la Porte Saint-Martin (10th *arrondissement*) in 1937.

AUGUST

August 14 – Ada "Bricktop" Smith, one of Montmartre's most popular performers and club owners of the 1920s jazz era (9th *arrondissement*), was born on this day in 1894.

August 17 – James Baldwin rallied support for the civil rights March on Washington at a meeting in a Paris jazz club called the Living Room (8th *arrondissement*) in 1963.

August 18 – Lieutenant James Reese Europe's 369th Infantry Regiment (World War I) jazz band performed at the Théâtre des Champs-Elysées (8th *arrondissement*) during the Conference of Allied Women in 1917.

ANNIVERSARY DATES . . . . CONTINUED

SEPTEMBER

September 21 – New Orleans-born playwright Victor Séjour died in a municipal hospital in Paris in 1874. He is buried in Père Lachaise cemetery (20th *arrondissement*).

September 28 – Victor Séjour's adaptation of Shakespeare's *Richard III* opened at the Théâtre de la Porte Saint-Martin (10th *arrondissement*) in 1852. As a result of its success, Séjour was proclaimed as being "among the most beloved of the young literary generation."

September 28 – Singer Marion Anderson gave a concert at Sainte-Chapelle (4th *arrondissement*) in 1965, the proceeds of which went to support the World Festival of Negro Arts in Dakar, Senegal.

OCTOBER

October 2 – Josephine Baker was catapulted to stardom after her opening as the star attraction of *La Revue Nègre* at the Théâtre des Champs-Elysées (8th *arrondissement*) in 1925.

October 19 – Sidney Bechet gave a free concert at the Olympia Music Hall (9th *arrondissement*) in 1955, at which his adoring French fans became so emotionally charged that they demolished the theater.

October 29 – Langston Hughes was honored by the French National Writers' Committee at the Hôtel Lutetia (6th *arrondissement*) in 1964.

NOVEMBER

November 13 – Paul Robeson was the guest of honor at a party given by Sylvia Beach, owner of the bookstore and lending library Shakespeare & Company (6th *arrondissement*), in 1925.

November 23 – Malcolm X addressed an audience at the Salle de la Mutualité (5th *arrondissement*) during a stopover from his second trip to Africa in 1964.

November 28 – Richard Wright died at the age of 52 in the Eugène Gibez clinic (15th *arrondissement*) in 1960. He lived and raised a family in Paris beginning in 1947.

DECEMBER

December 1 – Reginald Lewis, Harvard lawyer and business mogul, closed a billion dollar deal in 1987 and became the owner of TLC Beatrice, the French food conglomerate. In 1988 he moved his family to Paris, from where he ran his European headquarters.

December 14 – Josephine Baker opened her first nightclub, "Chez Josephine," in Montmartre (9th *arrondissement*) in 1926.

Stokely Carmichael spoke against the Vietnam War at the Salle de la Mutualité (5th *arrondissement*) in 1966.

Walks through African-American Paris

We are now ready to delve into the heart of the subject of this book – six walks through African-American Paris. Most of these walks take you through central Paris where visitors to the City of Light generally spend the majority of their time, and all present the areas where African Americans have been most active throughout the years.

At first glance Paris looks like a tangle of broad avenues and medieval streets, where people drive wildly and shops close at odd hours of the day. As a city subdivided into twenty very distinct *arrondissements* (districts), each with its own history, character, social classes, and cultural style, Paris feels more like a collection of small villages than one city. Indeed, the city and its residents can be complicated and filled with contradictions that at times seem without logic. But there **is** logic, at least in the layout of this beautiful town, and once you grasp it your visit to the City of Light will be enriched.

Paris unwinds in a clockwise spiral with the oldest and smallest *arrondissements* found in the center (Map 1). The first eight districts are distinguished by their presence on either the Left Bank or the Right Bank of the Seine River. Our walks take you to both the Left and Right banks, and two of them venture farther away from the Seine to neighborhoods that are not often visited by tourists. A brief description of each walk follows.

The Sorbonne / Mouffetard walk provides a tour of the 5th *arrondissement*. You will see the illustrious University of Paris

Sorbonne, learn a little about the ancient history of this area (it was settled by the Romans centuries ago), and visit one of Paris's most celebrated shopping streets, rue Mouffetard. Against this backdrop, you will learn about several African Americans who studied at the Sorbonne as well as see sites frequented by many of our artists and writers, including Aaron Douglas and Langston Hughes . You will also learn of a group of African-American high school students who performed in the revered Pantheon, and about the Nardal Sisters, black women from the Caribbean, who were instrumental in the launching of the *Négritude* movement (a cause devoted to affirming black culture through literature) in France.

The walk through Saint-Germain-des-Près (6th *arrondissement*) is circular, meaning that you begin and end in the same place. The world famous trio of cafés — the Deux Magots, the Flore, and the Brasserie Lipp — mark the starting point, and the importance of café life for African Americans is emphasized. You will work your way past the magnificent place Saint-Sulpice to the edge of the beautiful Luxembourg Garden, where you will see a major hangout for African Americans writers of the post-World War II era. A visit to the garden follows, then a walk past the theater where the great playwrights Alexandre Dumas and Victor Séjour saw their works performed. A stroll in a quarter where jazz was once king leads you back to the Café de Flore and the end of the tour.

The Saint-Michel / Musée d'Orsay walk takes you through the upper part of the 6th and 7th *arrondissements*. Here, the word "upper" means the part of the district that is closest to the Seine. Art galleries are prominent in this area of the 6th, and you will see many where African Americans exhibited their work. Additionally, you will be able to visit the shops of several dealers of African art and artifacts. Walking by the French Institute, you will learn of an African American who excelled as a Shakespearean actor in the nineteenth century. Moving on to the 7th *arrondissement*, you will discover more about many of our famous writers and painters while surveying the plethora of antique stores for which this quarter is known. You will end the walk at the museum dedicated to the Legion of Honor, where you will learn of several African Americans who received its prestigious award, and the Musée d'Orsay, which contains several works depicting people of color.

In Montparnasse (lower 6th and 14th *arrondissements*), the focus shifts to emphasize the lives and works of artists. While parts of this walk take you to areas frequented by tourists, you will also go into neighborhoods that are off the beaten path. Montparnasse has been steeped in artistic tradition since the early 1900s, and African-American artists such as Augusta Savage and Laura Wheeler Waring of the "Negro Colony" of the 1920s and 1930s and abstract artists Ed Clark and Beauford Delaney of the post-World War II era settled here in keeping with that tradition. You will see where they lived and worked, and visit the cafés that were as important to life in this district as were the Deux Magots and the Flore to life in Saint-Germain-des-Près. You will also see the famous Bobino Theater, where Josephine Baker made a triumphant comeback to the Paris stage and performed her last show ever, and the square that was dedicated in her honor.

Our Notre-Dame-de-Lorette / Opéra walk in the 9th *arrondissement* is another off-the-beaten-path walk that takes you to the area where African Americans first established a community in Paris after World War I. The night club scene is what made "Pig Alley" (a tortured pronunciation of Pigalle, the name of a street and a square found in the area) renowned in its day. Here you will learn about the players – Langston Hughes, Josephine Baker, and Bricktop were among them – who turned this district into "the Harlem of Paris." Leaving the Pigalle area and moving back toward an area more frequented by tourists, you will see the theater where Sidney Bechet inspired such a frenzy in his French audience that it rioted, and the opera house where W. E. B. Du Bois and Countee Cullen enjoyed performances.

The final walk presented in ***Paris Reflections*** covers the most well known and popular area of Paris, that of the Louvre (1st *arrondissement*) and the Champs-Elysées (8th *arrondissement*). Here you will see Paris in all of its grand style: the Tuileries Garden, place de la Concorde, the twin facades of La Madeleine church and the Assemblée Nationale, and the grandest of avenues – the Champs-Elysées – capped by the splendid Arc de Triomphe. A wide variety of African American activity took place here, from a civil rights march in support of Dr. King's March on Washington to a state funeral for Josephine Baker. Some of our artists' best works have been exhibited and honored with awards at the Grand Palais just off the Champs-Elysées. More recently, an African American left his indelible mark in the Louvre when he remodeled part of its recently renovated Richelieu wing. You will learn of all these things and more in the Louvre / Arc de Triomphe walk.

Each walk takes approximately 1½ hours to complete. If you are not familiar with negotiating the streets of Paris, please note that street signs are located on the walls of corner buildings, not on posts as they are in the US. Look for street numbers above or beside the principal entrances of buildings. Keeping these tips in mind will help eliminate frustration and allow you to concentrate more fully on the text.

There is no particular order in which to take these walking tours – simply go when and where the mood strikes you. No matter which ones you choose, you are sure to be amazed at the number and the variety of events and activities that African Americans have undertaken in the City of Light.

Sorbonne / Mouffetard Walk

The Ile de la Cité was occupied long ago by the Romans, who expanded their settlement onto the Left Bank of the Seine and up the hill now known as Montagne-Sainte-Geneviève. This area was known to the Romans as Lutetia. During this walk, you will see how African-American history unfolded on the same land developed by these ancient conquerors.

We begin at the metro Cluny-La Sorbonne (Map 2). Upon exiting the train, take the exit marked *Sortie 1* – boulevard Saint-Michel. When you exit the station, you will find yourself on the corner of boulevard Saint-Michel and boulevard Saint-Germain. Boulevard Saint-Michel was once a Roman *cardo*, or north-south thoroughfare, leading from the principal settlement on Ile de la Cité. On the southeast corner is the square Cluny, home to the medieval garden that so aptly complements the rear of the Musée du Moyen Age. This museum, formerly the residence of the abbey of Cluny, was built adjacent to the remains of the northern-most Roman baths of Lutetia. Walking up boulevard Saint-Michel, you can observe these ruins.

Retrace your steps to boulevard Saint-Germain and turn right. This thoroughfare, named for a bishop of Paris who lived during the Middle Ages, leads you immediately to the first stop on the tour. Walk east on boulevard Saint-Germain, noting the juxtapositioning of the Roman ruins and the Gothic/Renaissance architecture of the Museé de Moyen Age as you go. In the middle of the next block, stop at No. 71. Here stands FNAC, a branch of the mammoth CDvideo-computer-book emporium that is known throughout France. In 1992, this branch was an international bookstore. It hosted many of the writers who participated in a conference entitled "African Americans and Europe" that was held in February at the Sorbonne. A photo exhibit of African-American writers and artists who lived in Europe was displayed here as well. In 1993, Toni Morrison was an honored guest at the bookstore, and was invited to read from her various writings.

Continue to the corner, where boulevard Saint-Germain intersects with rue Saint-Jacques. Rue Saint-Jacques was the primary Roman *cardo*, with boulevard Saint-Michel representing a secondary north-south route from the Ile de la Cité. Turn right and walk up the street. At the first intersection (rue du Sommerard), look to your right to view from a different perspective the Hôtel de Cluny, the mansion that houses the Musée du Moyen Age. Note the gargoyles, serving as drain pipes for the roof above, that extend from the upper stories. While often modeled on dragons or other grotesque creatures, surrealist poet Ted Joans observed that one of the gargoyles here takes the form of two monks. He saw one of the monks as defecating, "hanging its . . . bare ass over the heads of millions yearly," while the second monk "frowns due to no one ever looking up." The Sorbonne, which had its origin as an open-air university, was founded on this street.

Continue up rue Saint-Jacques to the next intersection (rue des Ecoles) and turn right. Standing at the corner, look across the street. Here, spanning the entire block, you can see the facade of the famous Sorbonne. Several notable African Americans have studied here over the last two centuries. In just a few minutes you will have a view of its famous chapel and get a chance to look around its courtyard.

Proceed up rue des Ecoles (one of two remaining Roman *decumani*, or east-west thoroughfares), stopping briefly in front of square Paul Painlevé on the place of the same name. Here you have a full frontal view of the Musée du Moyen Age. Inside the gate to the left stands a sculpture of the wolf that suckled Romulus and Remus, symbolic of the founders of Rome. The offices of the publishing house Editions Liana Levi were once located at number 5 on the square – this company published some of the works of Ernest Gaines.

Cross the intersection at place Paul Painlevé and stand just opposite the Brasserie Balzar, which neighbors the Sorbonne at No. 49, rue des Ecoles. This restaurant retains its original quaint, cramped charm, even though it has now been purchased by the restaurant moguls the Blancs brothers *(les frères Blancs)*. Because it is in such close proximity to the university, it is not surprising that several participants of the first Congress of Negro Artists and Writers convened at the Sorbonne in 1956 by the *Société Africaine de Culture* (African Cultural Society) chose to meet here to debate issues. Richard Wright also dined here frequently in 1946 when he rented a room in which to type his manuscripts on nearby boulevard Saint-Michel.

Cross rue des Ecoles at its intersection with rue de la Sorbonne to walk past the Balzar. Continue to the next intersection, rue Champollion. Turn left next to the repertory theater on the corner and enter the street. At an unknown number on this street (possibly no. 3, 5, or 7) was once located a black-owned club and restaurant called Chez Inez. This club was run by jazz and blues singer Inez Cavanaugh from 1949-1952. Fried chicken was reportedly the specialty of the house. Farther up the street at No. 19, painter Aaron Douglas called the Hôtel Champollion home. While on a Julius Rosenwald scholarship, he studied art in the Montparnasse area (the subject of another walk in this book). The hotel has long since been replaced by private apartments and a bookstore on the ground level.

At the end of rue Champollion you enter the place de la Sorbonne. Turn left for a magnificent view of the seventeenth-century chapel of the Sorbonne, which is unfortunately no longer open to visits by the public except on special occasions. Built in the classic style, it houses Cardinal Richelieu's tomb. African-American art and photography were exhibited here in 1985 at an exposition entitled "The Atlanta in France." Atlanta Mayor Andrew Young and French Minister of Culture Jack Lang were present to open the event.

Proceed toward the chapel and turn left onto rue de la Sorbonne. At No. 17 is the entrance to the courtyard. Upon entering, you will see another view of the chapel to your right. White marks on the ground delineate the boundaries of the original college, which was founded by Robert Sorbon in 1253 on rue du Sommerard and moved to this site sometime afterward. As stated previously, many notable African Americans have studied here. Anna Julia Cooper rose from slavery to become the first African American to obtain a Ph.D. from this university in 1925, defending her dissertation at the age of 66! Carter G. Woodson, Countee Cullen, William Emmet Coleman, Gwendolyn Bennett, and Angela Davis are among many others who lingered in this courtyard and attended classes in these hallowed halls.

The Sorbonne has been the site for many events given for, by, and / or about African Americans. The 1992 conference "African Americans and Europe" has already been mentioned. In 1996, a conference on African-American music and Europe was co-sponsored by the W. E. B. Du Bois Institute of Harvard University and the Université de Paris III. In July 2000, Harvard professor Cornel West addressed a group of African Americans who gathered to celebrate the vibrant history of African Americans in Paris. And in October 2000, a conference on the African Diaspora included scores of African-American professors and scholars, as well as resident African Americans who provided entertainment and served as ambassadors of good will to visitors participating in the conference.

While the amphitheaters are likely to be occupied by students or closed to the public, a quick visit may be possible. When you come to the amphitheaters, gently try the doors and if they are open and unoccupied, take a look inside. Almost immediately opposite the entrance to the courtyard, look for the doors marked Joseph Victor Le Clerc and Victor Cousin. Entering either of these doors will take you into a corridor from which you can access the amphitheaters. The Richelieu amphitheater (straight ahead with entrances on either side of the stairwell) is where Anna Julia Cooper defended her dissertation on French policies concerning slavery during the Revolution. The Descartes amphitheater on the left was the site of the conference of black writers that was sponsored by the African Cultural Society *(Société Africaine de Culture)* mentioned previously. The Salle Louis Liard on the right is where Cornel West spoke in July 2000. And the Grand amphitheater (located in another area and generally closed to the public) was the site of the 1996 inaugural session of the conference "African-American Music and Europe."

Leaving the Sorbonne using the same route from which you came, turn left and walk past the chapel to enter rue Victor Cousin. At the first intersection is rue Cujas (the second of the two east-west roads used by the Romans). Turn right.

At No. 18 is the Hôtel Cujas Pantheon, formerly the Hôtel Logos. Langston Hughes was a guest in this hotel in August 1963. No. 20 is the Hôtel Excelsior, where painter Walter Coleman and cartoonist Ollie Harrington were guests during the 1950s.

Retrace your steps to rue Victor Cousin, cross the street, and continue up rue Cujas. You are now walking next to the south wall of the Sorbonne. At the next intersection you will find yourself once again at rue Saint-Jacques. Across the street and to the left, the long, impressive building is the Lycée (high school) Louis-le-Grand. This is one of the most prestigious high schools in Paris, where Aimé Césaire, widely considered to be the founder of the *Négritude* movement, was a student in 1931. It was here that he became friends with Léopold Sédar Senghor, the future president of Senegal.

Turn right and walk up rue Saint-Jacques to the first intersection, rue Soufflot. Turn left on rue Soufflot and admire the magnificent view of the Pantheon. The Duke Ellington High School of Performing Arts Jazz Band from Washington, DC performed here during the summer of 1999, as a stopover while on their way to a concert in the south of France.

Continue up the street to reach the place du Pantheon. Take the crosswalk to the right and stop for a second to peer in the windows of a gem of an old-time pharmacy located directly ahead at No. 3. Then follow the sidewalk around the square. The large building immediately to the right houses the *Mairie* (town hall) of the 5th *arrondissement*, or district. Among the functions of the *maire*, or mayor of the district, is to marry residents of the district. It was here that journalist Richard Gibson married his British fiancée in 1956. Continuing around the square, No. 19 is the Hôtel du Pantheon. Journalist Joel A. Rogers was a guest here in 1955-1956.

Continue around the square so that you may appreciate the architecture of the Pantheon from many sides. You can see traces of windows on the walls – forty-two of them were bricked up when this former church dedicated to Sainte-Geneviève (for whom the "mountain" that you are currently standing was named) was deconsecrated and devoted to the glory of French heroes. Napoleon converted it back to a church, followed by King Louis-Philippe who deconsecrated it once again. Napoleon III rededicated the building to Sainte-Geneviève, but with the coming of the Third Republic, the church was deconsecrated yet a third time. Today the Pantheon remains a temple to the glory of France, though the cross atop the dome remains as a sign of the time when the building was devoted to worship.

Still on the south side of the Pantheon, cross rue d'Ulm and look diagonally to the left for a view of the Tour Clovis, the last visible remnant of the medieval abbey church of Sainte-Geneviève. Continue around the square on the east side and walk to the corner. Here the place du Pantheon meets the place Sainte-Geneviève. Look at the apartment building across the street at No. 6. This is the building in which Caroline Dudley Reagan stayed when she brought Josephine Baker to Paris in 1925 to perform in *La Revue Nègre*.

Cross rue Clovis and walk past the church Saint-Etienne-du-Mont to enter rue de la Montagne-Sainte-Geneviève. Streets in this area have a medieval character, becoming narrow and winding. The first intersection on the right is the rue Descartes, and the building across the tiny square is the former home of the Ecole Polytechnique, a school of grand standing in France. This site was originally the home of the Collège de Navarre, one of the universities that sprung up on the Left Bank during medieval times. Follow rue Descartes, observing the gardens on the left as you head for place de la Contrascarpe.

The gardens end at rue Clovis. At this intersection, look to the right for a last glimpse of the Tour Clovis and the Pantheon. This stretch of rue Descartes is a former haunt of Ernest Hemingway and James Joyce. Note No. 42, a former address of the publishing house Présence Africaine. It was here that the *Société Africaine de Culture* was founded in September 1956. Josephine Baker and James Ivy were chosen as vice presidents by the Paris group, which elected Haitian Jean Price-Mars as its president. Richard Wright, Mercer Cook, and E. Franklin Frazier were among the nominees for the executive council.

Continue on rue Descartes, which changes into rue Mouffetard once you cross rue Thouin. At No. 6 on the right, observe the artistic cows and sheep affixed to the storefront. These indicate that this was once a butcher shop. Such imagery was heavily utilized during the Middle Ages, for the majority of the population could not read and needed signs or symbols to identify shops.

Just a few yards ahead lies place de la Contrascarpe. Take a moment to absorb the village-like atmosphere. Two huge cafés dominate this little square. Immediately to your left at No. 2-4 is the Café Delmas. This was formerly La Chope, one of writer Chester Himes' haunts when he lived in this neighborhood. William Gardner Smith also lived in the area and enjoyed La Chope as well. La Chope existed until late 2000; the contemporary style of the Café Delmas and the Café Contrascarpe across the square is for some an unwelcome contrast to the otherwise village-like surroundings.

At an unknown number on the square was a place called Café

Cinq Billiards, where surrealist poet Ted Joans once performed. To your right, at No. 14 rue Mouffetard, stands a grocery store above which hangs a sign that says *Au Nègre Joyeux* (Plate 1). Accompanying the sign is an image (currently undergoing restoration) of a black man serving a white woman a beverage. Centuries ago, the image of an African or a person of African descent was used on places of business to indicate that chocolate was sold or served there.

After a brief stroll around the square, take rue du Cardinal Lemoine to the right of Café Delmas and proceed to the first intersection on the right. At No. 74, on the left, is a plaque which indicates that Ernest Hemingway and his wife Hadley had an apartment here. The intersecting street is rue Rollin. Turn onto it and proceed to the end of the block. At No. 4, on the left, is the apartment building in which Oberlin College and Sorbonne scholar Anna Julia Cooper lived while preparing her dissertation.

Take the stairway at the end of rue Rollin down to rue Monge and cross this street. Turn left and proceed to No. 49. Here you enter the Arènes de Lutèce, another remnant of the Roman presence in Paris. John Paynter waxed poetic about this place during a visit to Paris, marveling at the "moss-covered walls" and the "iron-barred dungeon-like cages from which ferocious beasts may have been unleashed for the gory spectacles of Roman days." The Arènes are a peaceful haven and provide greenery and park benches, play areas for children, and a huge sandy surface for the diehard *pétanque* players who contribute to the romantic folklore of France.

Exit the arena to the right, entering rue de Navarre. Follow this street to the left (it immediately becomes rue des Arènes) and enter rue Linné. Turn right and walk down the street. At No. 5 is the Tim Hôtel Jardin des Plantes, where journalist John A. Williams stayed in June 1990.

At the intersection in front of the hotel, rue Linné, rue Cuvier, and rue Lacépède intersect. On the southeast corner of this intersection lies an entrance to the Jardin des Plantes. Abolitionist William

Wells Brown and A.M.E. Bishop Daniel A. Payne enjoyed this garden in the nineteenth century. Turn-of-the-century artist Henry O. Tanner, the trailblazer for African-American artists in Paris, often came here to sketch. In the 1930s, Joel A. Rogers and John Paynter frequented the grounds. Another oasis of calm in the chaotic city of Paris, this garden is worth a separate visit. But for now, cross the street and continue walking next to the garden wall.

The street name now changes to rue Geoffroy Saint-Hilaire. It was immortalized in a painting by renowned artist Loïs Mailou Jones. No. 51, on the right, was the home of the Achilles family. This Martinican family played host to John Paynter during his 1936 visit to Paris, and to Jones during her visit in 1937. The niece of Mme Achille was Paulette Nardal, one of the founders of the *Revue du Monde Noir* (Black World Review) and *L'Etudiant Noir* (The Black Student); she was an important intermediary between the Harlem Renaissance writers and the francophone university students of the time. Paulette and her sisters Jane and Andrée organized a literary salon and were also involved in the production of yet a third publication called *La Dépêche Africaine* (The African Dispatch). All three, but Paulette most of all, helped spawn the *Négritude* movement in France.

Beginning at No. 47, you can see the rear of one of the most unique sites in Paris, the Muslim Institute and Mosque. You will be able to take a closer look at this architectural marvel in just a few minutes. Immediately across the intersection with rue Daubenton is No. 35, where William Gardner Smith lived with his French wife Solange and their two children in 1967.

Cross the street at the crosswalk in front of the mosque. On the corner is the entrance to the graceful and charming Mosque Tea Room. You are transported into another world and another time when you stop here for North African pastries and a cup of tea. Roses and holly are among the plants that adorn the courtyard. The entrance to the *hammam*, used on alternate days by men and women, is also accessible from the courtyard.

Proceed down rue Daubenton. At the first intersection (rue Georges Desplas), look right for another view of the mosque. Continue down the street to its intersection with rue de la Clef. On the northwest corner stands Images d'Ailleurs, an *avant-garde* movie theater that specializes in films made by and for people of color. In 1992, in conjunction with the "African Americans and Europe" conference, an African-American film festival was held here. The theater also houses a conference room where discussions and debates are held. Julia Wright, Richard Wright's daughter, was instrumental in the staging of a meeting in defense of Mumia Abu-Jamal on this site in 1995. Melvin Van Peebles was the guest of honor at a conference when his movie *Sweet Sweetback's Baadasssss Song* was shown here.

Turn right onto rue de la Clef, walk to the first intersection, which is rue du Puit de l'Ermite, and turn right. Place du Puit de l'Ermite lies at the end of this street. At No. 1, place du Puit de l'Ermite, lies the front of the mosque. Here you have a full view of the entrance and the eighty-five-foot minaret tower. You may visit the main and inner courtyards, both of which allow you to appreciate the splendor of the work of the Tunisian, Moroccan, and Algerian artisans who created the Islamic motifs during the construction of the site in the 1920s. Educator John F. Matheus served as a guide to famous visitors Sir Arthur Conan Doyle and Karnac during their 1925 visit to the mosque.

Retrace your steps down rue du Puit de l'Ermite to its intersection with rue Monge. Turn right and walk down the street. On your left you will pass place Monge, a square where a lively open air market is held on Wednesdays, Fridays, and Sundays until about 1 PM. A short distance farther on rue Monge, writer and feminist critic Shirley Anne Williams stayed at No. 71, on the right, in 1992.

Retrace your steps to place Monge and cross rue Monge at rue Malus. Walk along the northern edge of the square to find rue Ortolan at its northwest corner. Walk down rue Ortolan to rue Mouffetard and turn right. In this block you come to No. 49 on the right, which was one of the former addresses of William Gardner Smith.

The next street on the right is rue Saint-Médard. In 1947, Loïs Mailou Jones captured the likeness of this intersection in her painting called *Coin de la rue Médard*. No. 38, rue Mouffetard, is just opposite the corner at rue Saint-Médard; it was once the home of a jazz club called The Blue Note. Notice that you are not far from place de la Contrascarpe, the square that you visited earlier in the walk. Turn around and retrace your steps to rue Ortolan, then continue walking down hill.

Rue Mouffetard is one of the best known market streets in Paris. It was built upon the track of an old Roman road leading south down Montagne-Sainte-Geneviève toward Italy. Though it has become somewhat of a tourist trap, particularly nearer place de la Contrascarpe, the atmosphere becomes more village-like as you descend the hill. Past a certain point, boutiques and Greek restaurants give way to a repertory theater, neighborhood cafés and *tabacs*, and vendors of cheeses, pastries, vegetables, and meats that continue to hold their own against the onslaught of commercialism. The surroundings become more and more picturesque, finally ending with a fountain and the medieval church Saint-Médard at the foot of the hill. The square Saint-Médard is the garden found adjacent to the fifteenth-century church of the same name.

This concludes the Sorbonne/Mouffetard walk. The nearest metro station is Censier-Daubenton.

Paris Reflections
Your Thoughts on the Sorbonne / Mouffetard Walk

Saint-Germain-des-Prés / Luxembourg — A Circular Walk

Cafés have been important for writers and artists in Paris for at least a century. They provided a warm, reasonably lit place to socialize, debate, and write when hotels in Paris (the primary abodes for writers and artists) were cold, poorly lit, and desolate. African-American artists and writers took advantage of cafés in this way, in both the Saint-Germain-des-Prés and Montparnasse areas. This walk explores Saint-Germain-des-Prés and the area adjacent to the Luxembourg Garden (Map 3). Here you will see many of the cafés that were so important to African-American writers, both socially and professionally.

The tour begins at the place Saint-Germain-des-Prés, where the medieval church of the same name stands. It was also called *Saint-Germain-le-Doré,* or the "golden Saint-Germain," due to the gilded roof that topped it during the Middle Ages. Henry O. Tanner made a sketch of the church, which can be viewed at the Smithsonian American Art Museum. Another representation of the church appears in the Cyrus Colter novel *Night Studies*.

Directly across from the church and in the corner of the square and boulevard Saint-Germain sits the Deux Magots café. This café and the neighboring Café de Flore and Brasserie Lipp are renowned for the intellectual crowd that they attracted from the 1920s through World War II. Les Deux Magots was one of Richard Wright's favorites. It was where James Baldwin (Plate 2) encountered Wright for the first time when Baldwin came to Paris in 1948. It was also the rendez-vous point for novelist Chester Himes' first meeting with his French translator, Yves Malartic. Directly across the boulevard is No. 149, now an Emporium Armani boutique. But in the days of Baldwin and Wright it was a bar called La Reine Blanche. This was a gay establishment that was described by painter Richard Olney as "a deep tunnel, lit brightly and crudely." Baldwin was a frequent customer, and it was here that he met his dear friend and lover Lucien Happersberger.

Walking along boulevard Saint-Germain in front of Les Deux Magots, you quickly reach rue Saint-Benoît. Standing on this corner, you have a clear view of the Café de Flore at No. 172, boulevard Saint-Germain and the Brasserie Lipp across the boulevard at No. 151. Baldwin used the upper room at the Flore to write; it was here that he completed *Go Tell It on the Mountain*. Some say that the famous argument between Baldwin and Richard Wright over the criticism Baldwin expressed about Wright's novel *Native Son* took place here as well, while others place the scene at the Lipp across the street. Baldwin achieved fame while living in Paris, in part because of the attention that he received as a result of his disagreement with Wright. He was eventually awarded the Legion of Honor by the French government because of his literary achievements. The upper room of the Flore is also the site where the Department of African-American Studies of Syracuse University held its first annual *Paris Noir* summer seminar on African-American history from June 2 through July 2, 2001.

Farther up the boulevard at No. 188 is the Café le Rouquet. Ted Joans, surrealist poet and artist, has adopted the Rouquet for daily gatherings with friends whenever he comes to Paris.

Cross boulevard Saint-Germain, turn left, and walk back down the boulevard until you reach the rue du Dragon. Turn right onto this street. At No. 3, on the left, was once the American Cultural Center in which former American Embassy exhibitions director Darthea Speyer had gallery space. Many African-American artists and writers were featured here, including Harold Cousins, Beauford Delaney, and Barbara Chase-Riboud. Farther up the street on the same side at No. 31 is the art academy Julian. Artists such as Henry O. Tanner, Loïs Mailou Jones, William Edouard Scott, Gwendolyn Bennett, and Palmer Hayden all received instruction here.

Rue du Dragon ends at the carrefour du Croix Rouge. Cross rue du Four, then turn right and proceed to rue du Vieux Colombier. Cross the street and turn left. No. 21 remains the address of the Théâtre du Vieux Columbier, where Chester Himes' German girlfriend Regine Fischer (a.k.a. Marlene Behrens in Himes' autobiography *My Life of Absurdity*) studied acting during the 1950s. It once housed the Club du Vieux Columbier, where master clarinetist Sidney Bechet and blues singer Inez Cavanaugh performed. Though the theater is still functional, the club is now gone.

Continue down rue du Vieux Colombier to rue de Rennes and turn right. No. 76, now the Cinéma l'Arlequin, was once the home of the jazz club La Rose Rouge. Maya Angelou and Billie Holiday both performed there during the 1950s. The club later changed hands and was renamed Le Timis. It then catered to an elite African crowd. The Timis no longer exists. A boutique owned by a man named Père Sauvage was once located at an unknown number on this street; Matisse purchased a piece of African art there and took it to Gertrude Stein's home. Picasso, who was heavily influenced by African art at one point in his career, saw the piece and was immediately enthused.

Retrace your steps to rue du Vieux Colombier and turn right. Cross rue de Rennes and walk to place Saint-Sulpice. The Eglise Saint-Sulpice was originally constructed as the parish church for the commoners who belonged to the Abbey Saint-Germain. Each of its towers has its own distinct characteristic – the northern one is four meters higher than the steeple at Notre-Dame and the shorter, southern one was never completed. While the church has never been considered one of beauty, it greatly inspired poet and artist Gwendolyn Bennett nonetheless during her visit to Paris in 1925. Duke Ellington gave a concert of sacred music here in 1969.

Cross the square diagonally from your point of entry to go to

No. 7, place Saint-Sulpice. The publishing house Editions Rieder used to be located here. Claude McKay and Langston Hughes were both published by Rieder in the late 1920s and 1930s.

The street exiting the square at this corner is rue Henry de Jouvenal. It quickly turns into to rue Ferou. Walking up the left side of the street, stop in front of 2 bis, rue Ferou, on the right side. In this old structure, you see a dilapidated wooden garage door and an angular extension of the main building with large, tall windows set back from the street on the first floor. It was here that surrealist photographer Man Ray had a studio. Ted Joans and many other African Americans were invited here by Ray during the early 1960s.

Retrace your steps back to the square, walk in front of the church, and turn right onto rue Saint-Sulpice. On the left, the Hôtel du Sénat can still be found at No. 22. William Gardner Smith and his female companion Ira Reuben were guests in this hotel; Smith completed his book *Return to Black America* here. James Baldwin also resided here for a time.

At the next intersection you will find rue de Seine on the left and rue de Tournon on the right. No. 1 rue de Tournon used to be the Hôtel de Tournon; it is now an apartment building. William Gardner Smith lived here with his wife Mary in 1951, and Smith lived here alone in 1961-1962. James Baldwin was a guest in this hotel in 1953.

Turn onto rue de Tournon and proceed up the street. At No. 18, the former Hôtel de Luxembourg was home to William Gardner Smith in 1955. On the ground floor at this address, the Café le Tournon still welcomes its customers. This café was one of the meccas for the African-American writers living in Paris in the 1950s and 1960s. It was "discovered" by Smith; Richard Wright, Leroy Haynes, Ollie Harrington, Chester Himes, Richard Gibson, and others soon became regular patrons as well. The Tournon was primarily a place for socializing and for picking up women. Chester Himes described it as "the most notorious interracial café in Europe," because most of the African-American men who came here consorted with white women.

The facade that you see at the end of rue de Tournon on rue de

Vaugirard is the Palais du Luxembourg, where the French Senate meets. It was originally the palace of Marie de Medici, the second wife of King Henri IV. You will see the front of the building a little later in the tour when you visit the Jardin du Luxembourg.

Turn right on rue de Vaugirard and proceed up the street. The first intersection on the right is rue Garancière. Editions Plon, one of Chester Himes' publishers, once had offices on this street. The next intersection is with rue Servandoni. After rue Servandoni you will see a crosswalk that leads to No. 19 on the left side of rue de Vaugirard. Take this crosswalk to stand before No. 19, the Musée du Luxembourg. In 1897, the French government purchased Henry O. Tanner's *The Raising of Lazarus* and had it displayed in this museum. Years later, Mary Church Terrell came to the museum expressly to see the painting, only to find that it had been removed and hung in the Louvre. Tanner's *Pilgrims at Emmaüs* also hung here once. Today the Musée du Luxembourg houses only temporary exhibitions.

To the right of the museum entrance is an entrance to the Jardin du Luxembourg. Many African Americans have found the garden inspiring, from Loïs Mailou Jones who captured its likeness on canvas in her work entitled *Dans le Jardin du Luxembourg* to Richard Wright and Bruce McMarion Wright who read and wrote here. Chester Himes and his girlfriend Regine would walk through this garden on their way to the Café Sélect in Montparnasse, where he wrote his novel *A Jealous Man Can't Win*.

Enter the garden and follow the path to the first major intersecting path to the left. Turn left to walk in front of the Orangerie and past the monument to Delacroix, then follow the curve of the path to the right to enter the area over which the front of the Palais du Luxembourg looks. As you round the curve you can see the dome of the Pantheon above the trees. Descend the steps to enter the clearing. Standing before the palace, you now have a view of the front of the building that you saw from the corner of rue de Tournon and rue de Vaugirard.

Marie de Medici, who became a widow after the assassination

of her husband, King Henri IV, commissioned the building of this palace in the likeness of the Pitti Palace in Florence, her original home. Though it bears little resemblance to the Pitti, the palace is an extravagant piece of architecture that took fifteen years to complete. After a succession of royal and aristocratic owner-occupants, it was made into a prison during the Revolution. It only became the seat of the Sénat in 1852. The president of the Sénat lives in a mansion located 1 in the garden found at No. 17, rue de Vaugirard.

Reverend Daniel Payne visited the palace in 1868 and Frederick Douglass attended a Sénat session here in 1886. Composer and pianist Philippa Schuyler had the occasion to practice piano here in 1955, when Gaston Monnerville of French Guiana served as Sénat president. Schuyler was a guest of the president's wife. In February 1994, the palace was the venue for a conference entitled "A Visual Arts Encounter: African Americans and Europe." It was jointly sponsored by the Contemporary Transatlantic Arts Program, the Center for Afro-American Studies at the Sorbonne, and other institutions. Raymond Saunders of the Contemporary Transatlantic Arts Program and Marie-Françoise Sanconie of the Franco-American Center in Paris were instrumental in its planning and implementation. Fifteen African-American artists and photographers were invited to participate, among whom were Faith Ringgold, Jacob Lawrence, and Lorna Simpson.

Continue on the path next to the palace to visit the grotto containing the Fontaine de Médicis, a famous trysting spot for Parisians. Then retrace your steps to the clearing, walking by the boat basin and observing the vista along rows of trees that lead your gaze to the observatory that stands well beyond the garden to the south. Then take the main pathway out of the garden to place Edmond Rostand.

At place Edmond Rostand, look across the intersection to rue Gay Lussac to see the Café au Départ. This is where Chester Himes wrote his novel *Pinktoes* in 1956. Himes became a celebrity in Paris because of the widespread acceptance of his Harlem detective novels, including *For Love of Imabelle* and *A Rage in Harlem*. Most of these were first published in France, beginning in the late 1950s.

Turning left on the sidewalk by the garden, follow it to rue de Médicis. As you walk, look to the left to see the rear of the Fontaine de Médicis within the garden gate. When you reach the end of rue de Médicis, you will be at place Paul Claudel. The large building across the street is the rear of the Odéon theater, which you will see more of in a moment.

Cross rue de Médicis and rue de Vaugirard to enter rue Corneille. Walking up this street you come to the place de l'Odéon, from where you can see the front of the theater. During the nineteenth century, Ira Aldridge played Othello here and received rave reviews. Alexandre Dumas' *Christine à Fontainebleau* and Victor Séjour's *André Gérard* were performed here in 1830 and 1857, respectively. Around the square are various places of interest. Looking down rue de l'Odéon immediately in front of the theater, the odd numbers are on the right and the even ones on the left. No. 1 was the site of the Centre Franco-Américain, where part of the James Hatch and Camille Billops Archives on African-American artists was exhibited in 1984. Before this, the address was home to the Odéon Cultural Center and even earlier, the Café Voltaire that was once frequented by Renoir and Gauguin. No. 2 is still the address of La Méditerranée, a favorite restaurant of Richard Wright. No. 6 is the address of the Michelet-Odéon hotel. It was formerly called the Hôtel Michelet, where Chester Himes met Willa Thompson in 1953.

Rue Casimir Delavigne is the street immediately to the right of rue de l'Odéon. Take this street to leave the square. At No. 8 on the left is La Cambuse, a restaurant that was once run by a friend of Richard Wright. At No. 3, the Hôtel des Grands Balcons was frequented by author Ernest Gaines. And at Hôtel Delavigne, at No. 1, Richard Wright booked a room for Chester Himes in 1953.

At the corner, on the right, is the Librairie de l'Escalier at No. 12, rue Monsieur le Prince. Richard Wright held a book signing here in 1959 in honor of the French publication of *White Man, Listen*. Cross the street, turn right, and proceed up rue Monsieur le Prince to the apartment building at No. 14 (on the right). A plaque on the wall to the left of the entrance commemorates Richard Wright, who made his home here for much of the time that he lived in Paris. It is the only plaque in Paris that pays tribute to an African American.

Richard Wright might well be considered the prince among African-American writers in Paris during the 1950s and 1960s. He was frequently sought out by the press to speak on the treatment of blacks in the United States, and was often in the company of the celebrated French existentialists Jean-Paul Sartre and Simone de Beauvoir. On his first visit to Paris in 1946 he was aided by none other than Gertrude Stein, who had a friend escort him to the Hôtel Trianon on rue de Vaugirard (not on this tour) where she had booked a room for him. Wright in turn helped many other African-American writers, including James Baldwin, whether they came to Paris to visit or to live.

Retrace your steps up the street and continue to No. 5, Le Comptoir du Relais. This was formerly the Café Monaco, one of Richard Wright's favorites due to its atmosphere and its proximity to his home. Wright introduced his friends to the Monaco after having moved down the street. The Monaco and the Tournon were the two principal cafés where African-American men congregated during the fifteen years following World War II.

You are now at the carrefour de l'Odéon. Turn right at the corner just past the old Monaco and walk to boulevard Saint-Germain. Cross the boulevard to enter rue de l'Ancienne Comédie. At No. 13, on the right, is the Café Procope, the first café ever opened in Paris. A site of historic significance for both French and Americans (French revolutionaries met and Benjamin Franklin drafted the alliance between France and the American Republic here), it was yet another favorite of Richard Wright. Marble plaques affixed to the building's facade recount some of the café's history.

Rue de l'Ancienne Comédie ends at a five-point intersection. To the left is rue de Buci. Turn onto this street and view the remarkable flower shop, gastronomic boutiques, and cafés that line it as you proceed to rue de Seine, the second intersection on the left. Turn onto rue de Seine and walk the short distance to No. 60 on the right. The Hôtel La Louisiane was not only home to French intellectual Simone de Beauvoir, but also to poet Bruce McMarion Wright and musicians Lester Young, T-Bone Walker, and Bud Powell. It was here that the 1986 movie *Round Midnight*, depicting the Parisian life of African-American jazzmen during the 1960s, was filmed.

Retrace your steps to rue de Buci and turn left. Almost immediately you will see No. 22, the Hôtel Buci, on the right side of the street. Now a four-star hotel, it was only a one-star establishment in 1969 when a brawl involving musicians Frank Wright, Muhammad Ali, Alan Silva, Noah Howard, and the hotel desk attendant broke out here over a mispronounced word. On the left, the café L'Arbuci has taken over the space that was once the Hôtel Jeanne d'Arc (formerly at No. 27). It was here where Chester Himes and his girlfriend Regine Fischer stayed in 1956 before moving to the Hôtel Rachou closer to the Seine.

Rue Bourbon-le-Château forms a T-intersection with rue de Buci just across the street from L'Arbuci. Turn onto this street. At No. 3 on the left, Chester Himes and his future wife Lesley Packard occupied a charming flat on the seventh floor in 1964. Himes described it as having "a large railed balcony which held six or eight chairs with a clear view of the nearby park and Saint-Germain-des-Prés at the end of rue de l'Abbaye." Among their visitors were Malcolm X, artist Herbert Gentry, and film-maker Melvin Van Peebles.

Rue Bourbon-le-Château continues into rue de l'Abbaye. As you enter this street you will notice the immense Abbatial Palace on the left, a reminder that this district was developed into a powerful abbey during the Middle Ages when it was under the jurisdiction of the Bishop of Paris, Saint-Germain. No. 6 on the right was once the home of the Cabaret de l'Abbaye, a nightspot run by Gordon Heath from 1948 to 1976.

Continue up rue de l'Abbaye, cross place Saint-Germain-des-Prés, and enter rue Guillaume Apollinaire. This short street leads to rue Saint-Benoît. Turn right and go to No. 7 on the right side of the street. Now the Hôtel Bel Ami, this building was once occupied by the Hôtel Latitudes. Latitudes housed a very popular jazz club for several years. No. 7 was also once home to the soul food restaurant Jezebel's, which opened in 1990. Alberta Wright, a *restaurateur* from South Carolina who runs the original Jezebel's in New York City, regaled her upscale Paris clientele here with African-American fare until 1994.

Retrace your steps to the corner of rue Guillaume Apollinaire and cross this street. On the corner at No. 13 is the club Le Bilboquet, the only jazz club remaining on rue Saint-Benoît that is open to the public. The small black door a little farther down is the entrance to the private Club Saint-Germain. This was once a jazz club featuring big name artists such as Duke Ellington, Charlie Parker, Miles Davis, Kenny Clarke, and Sidney Bechet. The Bilboquet began featuring live jazz during the 1960s when the Club Saint-Germain ceased to do so.

Across the street at No. 24 is the Hôtel Crystal. Singer Inez Cavanaugh, musicians Dexter Gordon and Don Byas, educator Mercer Cook, and poet Bruce McMarion Wright all called the Crystal home at some point during their sojourns in Paris. At No. 28 is the Montana Bar, where James Baldwin met his friend Mary Painter during the time that he was writing *Go Tell It on the Mountain*.

Continuing up rue Saint-Benoît, you rapidly come back to boulevard Saint-Germain and the Café de Flore. This marks the end of the tour. The nearest metro station is Saint-Germain-des-Prés, on boulevard Saint-Germain along the side of the church.

Paris Reflections
Your Thoughts on the Saint-Germain-des-Prés / Luxembourg Walk

Saint-Michel / Musée d'Orsay Walk

This walk emphasizes some of the successes of African-American artists and writers who have taken inspiration from the freedom and beauty that they experienced in Paris. Magnificent vistas from the quays of the Left Bank punctuate the route, which takes you through enchanting medieval streets and broader thoroughfares lined with *hôtels particuliers* (mansions), art galleries, antique shops, and restaurants.

Begin at metro Cluny-La Sorbonne (Map 4). To exit the station, take *Sortie 1* boulevard Saint-Michel. Once you reach the sidewalk, go to the corner directly ahead and turn right onto boulevard Saint-Michel. Proceed to place Saint-Michel and cross the boulevard to the left to stand in the center of the square.

This nineteenth-century square, dominated by the fountain that depicts a triumphant Saint Michael, has been a traditional meeting place on the Left Bank for centuries. The inscriptions on the squat pillars supporting the mythical beasts to either side of the fountain commemorate the inhabitants of the 5th and 6th *arrondissements* who gave their lives in the struggle to liberate Paris in 1944. Facing the river, you have a marvelous view of the Palais de Justice (the law courts) and the delicate spire of Sainte-Chapelle Cathedral rising above the palace walls.

Cross the square and the street that borders it so that you end up on the opposite side of place Saint-Michel. Walk toward the river. As you approach the quai des Grands Augustins, the busy thoroughfare that runs next to the river, you will see the *bouquinistes* (book vendors) along the river and Notre-Dame Cathedral across the river to the right. These are two quintessential elements of central Paris.

Turn left at the corner and go one block to rue Gît-le-Cœur. Turn onto this street. No. 9 on the left, now the four-star Hôtel du Vieux Paris, was once the Hôtel Rachou. Detective novelist Chester Himes and his girlfriend Regine Fischer stayed here in the late 1950s. Himes wrote the detective story *The Five-Cornered Square* (French version – *La Reine des Pommes*) in one of the front rooms here. This book was awarded the French Grand Prize for Detective Literature in 1958. The Rachou became known as a hangout for "beatniks" in the late 1950s, and surrealist poet and plastic artist Ted Joans came here in 1960 because of this reputation. Vertamae Grosvenor, a self-described "poet, actress, culinary anthropologist and writer" was also once a guest at the Rachou.

Proceed down rue Gît-le-Cœur to rue Saint-André-des-Arts. Turn right. The second intersection on the right is rue des Grands Augustins. Enter this street and proceed to the first intersection on the left. This is rue Christine. Turn onto this street. No. 2 on the right houses the offices of Editions de la Martinière. This organization has several publishing companies, among them Editions Minerva. Minerva is the publisher of *La Cuisine Noire Américaine,* the French version of the soul food cookbook, *Food for the Soul*, written by Monique Y. Wells and illustrated by Christiann Anderson. This book was written from the perspective of an African American living in Paris who began to crave food from her Texas and Louisiana family shortly after moving to the French capital. No. 6, now the bookstore for Editions de la Martinière, was once the Hôtel Christine. James Baldwin and musician Albert Nicholas once stayed here. Across the street at No. 5 was the home that Gertrude Stein and Alice B. Toklas shared when they returned to Paris after World War II. Richard Wright was a frequent guest here. It was Stein who arranged to have the French government extend an official invitation to Wright to come to France.

Proceed to the end of the street, where it intersects with rue Dauphine. On the corner is No. 33, the Café Laurent, part of the four-star Hôtel d'Aubusson. This site was the home of the Tabou Club, a jazz club that became famous for its jam sessions after the Nazis occupied Paris during World War II. It was a rather shabby place when it opened in 1947, but it attracted the *crème de la crème* of Paris intellectuals and featured French jazzman Boris Vian as the leader of the band. Though jazz had been banned by the Germans during the war because of its "degrading" influence, it went underground and emerged, vibrant as ever, in the post-war years.

Turn left on rue Dauphine and proceed to the corner where it intersects with rue Mazarine and rue de Buci to the right and rue Saint-André-des-Arts to the left. No. 65, rue Saint-André-des-Arts (across the street and just next to the corner boutique) once housed the jazz club called the Riverboat. It featured live music. One of its renowned guests was pianist Don Ewell, who regaled audiences in 1971. The site changed management and eventually closed in 1977. A Haitian art gallery, Galerie Antoinette Jean, now occupies the premises.

Cross rue Saint-André-des-Arts, turn left, and walk to the archway at No. 61 that leads into the Cour de Commerce Saint-André. Partially covered in the style of the fashionable *passages* of Paris, this historic alleyway was opened in 1776 and was frequented by the likes of Benjamin Franklin, Voltaire, and Robespierre. The seeds of the French revolution were sown and fruits of the American revolution were reaped at the Procope (the first Parisian café) that is still found in this alley. The guillotine, the latest innovation for public executions at the time, was perfected here. The Procope was one of Richard Wright's favorite cafés. A stroll down the passage and back will allow you to experience all of its charm.

Once back at the archway, look across the street. You can see the Hôtel Saint-André-des-Arts at No. 66. Chester Himes stayed here with Regine Fischer in 1958.

Retrace your steps to the intersection you just left and enter rue Mazarine, the second street to your right. You will note that the medieval character of the surroundings has given way to a more artsy atmosphere with galleries and restaurants. And at the end of the street, you can see a huge dome. You will discover the building to which it belongs a little later in the tour.

On the left side of the street at No. 62 stands L'Alcazar, a restaurant-bar that offers the utmost in trendiness in terms of both music and food. Promoting "good food all day and quality soulful sounds" and providing space for artists to display their work, the restaurant remains true to its history. It was here that the show *Harlem Black Birds, 1936* played during that same year; Duke Ellington performed here for a benefit supporting the French Artists' Union in 1969. Painter Arthur Beatty had an exhibition here in 1983.

At the next intersection, you will find rue Guénégaud on the right and rue Jacques Callot on the left. Turn right onto rue Guénégaud. No. 15 on the right was once the Paris address of the Hours Press, a publishing company owned and operated by British heiress Nancy Cunard beginning in 1929. She had a long relationship with Henry Crowder, who was an accomplished musician and songwriter. Crowder worked at the press, printing Samuel Beckett's *Whoroscope*. The Hours Press also published several of Crowder's songs in a book entitled *Henry-Music*. The grand *hôtel particulier* just opposite is the Hôtel de Monnaie de Paris, originally the national mint but now a coin museum and boutique.

On rue Guénégaud, near its intersection with rue Mazarine, are several galleries that sell African art and artifacts. These shops call to mind the tremendous influence that African art forms had on Picasso, Braque, Matisse, and other artists in Paris at the beginning of the twentieth century, as well as the inspiration that African-American artists in Paris took from African art during the Harlem Renaissance years. Take a little time to browse as you retrace your steps to the intersection. No. 31 near the corner was once the Galerie Karin Moutet. In 1961, Walter Coleman exhibited his portraits of Billie Holiday here.

At the intersection, cross rue Mazarine and enter rue Jacques

Callot. Opera lovers will be interested to know that on this corner, where Le Bistrot Mazarin now stands, the first Paris opera house was opened in 1671. Ted Joans first encountered famous photographer Man Ray on this street, and captured the meeting in a poem. At No. 6, Darthea Speyer continues her support of American artists in Paris at her gallery. She was the inspiration behind the now defunct American Cultural Center in another area of the 6th *arrondissement*, where she took an interest in Beauford Delaney's work in 1961. She holds selected pieces of Delaney's work at her current address, and also has some of painter Sam Gilliam's works. She has featured both artists at exhibitions in her gallery.

No. 10-12, Galerie Pierre Robin and No. 3, Galerie O. Klejman and Stella L. are yet additional vendors of tribal art and artifacts. A curious statue sits in front of No. 16. It consists of alternating slices of a black woman and a white woman with a cello, an artist's palette, paint brushes, a stack of books, a pipe, and a broken picture frame combining to make a surrealistic whole. Called the *Venus des Arts* (1988), this is the work of the French artist Arman, who was also influenced heavily by African art. On the corner is the well known café La Palette. It was a favorite hangout of jazz musicians Anthony Braxton and Marion Brown during the late 1960s.

At the end of this block you come to rue de Seine. Turn right and proceed up the right side of the street; this section dates back to the thirteenth century. Looking at the buildings on the left, note the relief of a black man on the wall of the first story of the building at No. 26. The inscription says AU PETI MAURE. This building was once the site of a cabaret called Le Petit-Maure (The Little Moor) where many renowned writers drank during the seventeenth century. No. 31 was formerly the home of George Sand; during the 1920s, it was the site of the Académie Raymond Duncan, owned by the brother of Isadora Duncan. Anne Coussey was a student at the Académie in 1924 when she met Langston Hughes (Plate 3); the two eventually became a couple. An exhibition called "American Painters in Paris" was held here in 1951, and Michael Kelly Williams was one of the artists featured. Oliver Harrington, cartoonist for the *Pittsburg Courier*, was a tenant of Raymond Duncan during the 1950s.

Almost directly across the street at No. 20 is the Galerie Zlotowski. This address was formerly the home of the Galerie Resche, where between 1990 and 1992 Raymond Saunders had two one-man exhibitions of his paintings, Ed Clark had one such show, and Saunders, Clark, and Sam Middleton held a joint exhibit. The Galerie Resche was also the site chosen for a joint exhibition of African-American artists during the 1994 conference "A Visual Arts Encounter: African Americans and Europe." At No. 12, Henry O. Tanner rented a ground-floor studio apartment in 1891. He later moved across the street to No. 15. Larry Potter had his works exhibited on this street at the now defunct Galerie de la Librairie Anglaise (address unknown) in 1964.

Continuing down the street, you will see square Henri Champion on the left, and an archway just opposite on the right. Go through the arch and you will find yourself at place de l'Institut. You now have a close-up view of the building that houses the Institut de France, the dome of which you saw from rue Mazarine.

This institute is the home of five prestigious academies, each specializing in a different area: L'Académie Française (French language), l'Académie des Inscriptions et Belles-Lettres (history), l'Académie des Sciences (science), l'Académie des Beaux-Arts (art) and l'Académie des Sciences Morales et Politiques (political sciences). It was founded in 1795 and was originally located in the Louvre. In 1805 Napoleon had it moved to this site. The building that you see was originally home to a college established at the behest of Mazarin in the seventeenth century; it served as a prison during the Revolution. Mazarin's tomb rests under the magnificent dome that covers the chapel.

In the late nineteenth century, a man named J. A. Arneaux, born in Georgia of a French father and a black mother of French descent, attended lectures at the Académie des Inscriptions et Belles-Lettres and the Académie des Sciences Morales et Politiques. He returned to the US and became a Shakespearean actor, playing to appreciative audiences and critics in New York City, Providence, RI, and Philadelphia, PA. He founded a troop of black Shakespearean actors called the Astor Place Tragedy Company, which appeared at several of the leading theaters in New York. He also worked as a journalist, then as a newspaper editor and publisher in New York between 1884 and 1886. In this role, he was perhaps the first to advocate renouncing the use of the word "color" for black Americans, preferring the term "Africo-American" instead. Successful as he was, he decided at the age of 32 to leave professional life to return to Paris to continue his studies.

Looking across the river, you have a splendid view of the Louvre directly opposite and of the wooden Pont des Arts, one of two pedestrian bridges to cross the Seine. To the right you can see the tower of the Eglise Saint-Germain l'Auxerrois (the former royal parish church just across from the Louvre) and the department store Samaritaine on the Right Bank.

From the place de l'Institut, turn left and follow the sidewalk to the next intersection on the left. This is rue Bonaparte. On the right at No. 8 is the Galerie 1900-2000. Ted Joans exhibited a work here in 1991 entitled *Estrus, or My Thing is Bigger Than His*. It was also on this street that Joans met André Breton, whom Joans admired greatly as a surrealist. Joans officially became a part of Bréton's surrealist movement, and the two became very good friends. Farther down the street at No. 14 is the Ecole des Beaux-Arts. For centuries, this school provided the most prestigious and classical education that an artist could have hoped for, and it continues to educate art students today. Many African Americans have studied here since the early nineteenth century; among them were Jules Lion, Charles Ethan Porter, Meta Vaux Warrick Fuller, Elizabeth Prophet, and Palmer Hayden. The New Orleans-born Lion showed many of his works in the acclaimed Paris art salons while a student here; in 1833 he won an honorable mention for his lithograph entitled *Affûts aux Canards*. But other African-American artists were disenchanted with the formality and rigidity of the school, and chose to attend the more *avant-garde* Académie de la Grande Chaumière and Académie Colarossi that are located in the Montparnasse area.

At this intersection you have reached the rue des Beaux-Arts. Turn left onto this street and proceed to No. 12 on the left. This is the Galerie Albert Loeb, where artist Romare Bearden held his first one-man show in Paris. Galerie Craven, one of the first American art galleries in Paris, was also located on the rue des Beaux-Arts. Sylvester Britton and Ed Clark had exhibitions at the Craven in 1953.

Across the street at No. 13 is the Hôtel des Beaux-Arts. It was here that in 1954 James Baldwin reportedly "hustled" money from Marlon Brando so that he could travel back to the United States. This was also the site where Oscar Wilde died (note the plaque affixed to the wall of the building to the left of the entrance).

Retrace your steps to rue Bonaparte and turn left. Proceed up the left side of the street. At No. 13 is a boutique called L'Ile du Démon. Formerly an art gallery (and still under the same management), this is the site where in 1982, Arthur Beatty exhibited his series of paintings of musicians entitled "Jazz Visuals." In the window to the right of the entrance is a photo of Nancy Cunard, companion of Henry Crowder and owner of the Hours Press. This photo was taken by Man Ray and was featured on the cover of Henry Crowder's song book *Henry-Music*.

Continue up the street to rue Jacob. Next door to the boutique on the southeast corner is the hotel La Villa (No. 29, rue Jacob). This hotel had an excellent jazz club for many years. This address was an important one for James Baldwin; the offices of *Zero* magazine were located here from 1949-1951. In June 1949, this journal published Baldwin's "Everybody's Protest Novel," the essay that criticized Richard Wright's writings and led to a feud between them.

43

Cross rue Bonaparte and proceed down rue Jacob to the right. No. 36 was one of the many sites in Paris at which Patricia Laplante held her African-American Literary Soirées. Farther down, the Hôtel d'Angleterre at No. 44 was a favorite of Chester Himes. No. 48 was the residence of James Baldwin in 1951. No. 56 is the place where Benjamin Franklin signed the treaty with England that granted the United States its independence. And the Hôtel du Danube at No. 58 was where filmmaker Madison D. Lacy stayed during his visits to Paris in 1991 and 1992.

At the end of the street, rue Jacob intersects with rue des Saints-Pères. This street serves as the border between the 6th and 7th *arrondissements*, and the eastern border of the *"Carré Rive Gauche,"* the charming and expensive antique market area of Paris.

Turn right onto rue des Saints-Pères, walk down to the second intersection on the left and turn onto rue de Lille. You will note that the architecture in this area has changed to one of elegance and refinement, reflecting the tastes of the nobles and bourgeois French who originally lived in the district. At No. 9, Richard Wright and his wife Ellen sublet a room in 1947. No. 17 was once home to the Galerie Paul Facchetti, where Beauford Delaney had an exhibition in 1960. Farther down on the opposite side of the street at No. 40, the Hôtel de Lille still stands. It was here, in a room on the top floor, that Richard Wright wrote *The Outsider*.

Proceed to the corner of rue de Lille and rue de Beaune, and turn left. Cross across the intersection with rue de l'Université, where rue de Beaune changes names to become rue Sébastien-Bottin. At No. 5 are the offices of the publishing house Editions Gallimard. Chester Himes, James Baldwin, Richard Wright, and John Edgar Wideman each had some of his literary works published by this firm.

Rue Montalembert begins just in front of Editions Gallimard. Walking up the left side of this very short street, you will pass the Hôtel Montalembert, the rear entrance of the Eglise de Saint-Thomas-Aquin, and the restaurant Les Antiquaires to reach No. 7, the entrance to the Hôtel du Port Royal. This hotel has been named the *Hôtel Litteraire*, or Literary Hotel, because of all the famous writers who have stayed here. Jean-Paul Sartre and Simone de Beauvoir are among the most well known French writers and intellectuals who frequented this place. Once James Baldwin became successful, this was also his favorite hotel. Chester Himes and his wife Lesley stayed here during June 1970 when they returned from Spain for a promotional visit arranged by Gallimard to coincide with the successful release of the movie *Cotton Comes to Harlem*. Himes's agent, Roslyn Siegel Targ, stayed at the Hôtel Montalembert during this time.

From the sidewalk in front of the Hôtel du Port Royal, look across the street that intersects with rue Montalembert. This is rue du Bac. At No. 42 is Galerie Maeght. Romare Bearden exhibited here in 1947 in a rare presentation of American art. One of the works that he displayed, *Blue Note*, was reproduced in the renowned Paris art journal *Cahiers d'Art*. The painter Al Loving was also featured in the exhibition "Living American Artists" at this gallery in 1975.

Retrace your steps and take the crosswalk that is in front of the restaurant Les Antiquaires; proceed to rue du Bac and follow it to rue de Verneuil. This area of the 7th *arrondissement* was known as "Musketeer country." The barracks of the seventeenth-century soldiers known as the Grey Musketeers were once situated in this vicinity, and their commander d'Artagnan lived at No. 1, rue du Bac. These soldiers were the inspiration for Alexandre Dumas's novel *The Three Musketeers*.

Turn left onto rue de Verneuil. This section of the street is called *"le hameau de Verneuil"* (the hamlet of Verneuil) because of the village-like atmosphere that the food shops on the first part of the block create. Androuët, the cheese shop at No. 37 on the left, is arguably the finest in Paris. Proceed to No. 53 to see the Hôtel d'Avejean. Once owned by the Musketeer the Marquis d'Avejean, this mansion now houses the Maison des Ecrivains (Writers' House) and the National Center for Books. These are sponsored by the

French Ministry of Culture. During the 1992 conference on African Americans and Europe, several African-American writers met here to discuss African-American fiction. Among them were Barbara Chase-Riboud, Ernest Gaines, Ishmael Reed, and Shirley Anne Williams. A very inviting café, Le Café des Lettres, is found in the courtyard of this magnificent *hôtel particulier*, and is open to all.

Continue to the end of the street where it intersects rue de Poitiers. Turn right and follow the street to rue de Lille. Turn left and continue to rue de Bellechasse. Cross the street and walk to No. 64 to stand before the grillwork that protects the courtyard of the Palace of the Legion of Honor. Numerous African Americans have received the Legion of Honor, one of the most illustrious awards bestowed by the French government. Among those so honored are Henry Ossawa Tanner, Josephine Baker, James Baldwin, Jessye Norman, Melvin Van Peebles, and Barbara Hendricks. Unfortunately, there is no listing of the honorees (French, American, or otherwise) inside the museum. The entrance to the museum is on rue de Bellechasse.

Retrace your steps to rue de Bellechase and turn left. The street now becomes a pedestrian walkway called rue de la Legion d'Honneur. Walk to the end of the street for a final view of the Louvre, which is across the Seine to the right. Then turn back and mount the steps on your left to stand before the Musée d'Orsay. This building, one in which the city of Paris takes great pride, was originally constructed to function as a train station and hotel near the grounds of the huge fair held in 1900 – the *Exposition Universelle* (Universal Exposition or World Fair). It was closed in 1973, and saved from demolition by the outcry raised by Parisians concerned with preserving the architectural heritage of the city. Thus the old train station was renovated and made into the museum that millions enjoy today.

In addition to the Impressionist paintings, statuary and *maquettes* from the Palais Garnier, and other pieces in this museum, there are numerous works of art that depict Africans or people of

African descent. The statue representing Africa that is found in the row of sculptures at the edge of the plaza in front of the museum (made for the *Exposition Universelle* of 1878) is one example. Lunch can be enjoyed at a neighborhood café or inside the museum (perhaps in the well preserved *Belle Epoque* hotel dining room), followed by a leisurely stroll through the magnificent rooms. Alternatively, you may decide to return to the museum another day and allow more time for a thorough visit.

This marks the end of the place Saint-Michel / Musée d'Orsay walk. The nearest public transportation stations are the RER C, just beneath the museum, and the metro Solferino, a few blocks away on boulevard Saint-Germain.

Paris Reflections
Your Thoughts on the Saint-Michel / Musée d'Orsay Walk

Montparnasse Walk

Montparnasse, the longtime Bohemian capital of Paris, is a place where African Americans have sought instruction in the plastic arts since early in the twentieth century. From the late great masters Henry O. Tanner and Loïs Mailou Jones to successful contemporaries such as abstractionist Ed Clark, dozens of African Americans have lived and studied here. This walk will explore their haunts, as well as those of many other people of African descent.

We begin at place du 18 juin 1940, through which boulevard du Montparnasse runs in a northwest-southeast direction (Map 5). If you have arrived by metro at the Montparnasse-Bienvenüe station, take *Sortie* (exit) *5*, boulevard du Montparnasse or *sortie 8*, rue de Rennes, to leave the station. Once you reach the top of the stairs, you will easily spot the square to the south of the boulevard. Turn to face it and take in the scene, which is reminiscent of a mini-New York City with its huge video screen affixed above the shopping center, the skyscraper behind it, the advertisements found everywhere (at night all ablaze in neon), and the crowds of people. During the 1960s, much of this area was bulldozed and rebuilt around the train station located behind the tower, the Tour Montparnasse. While the old district had become quite dilapidated, it was destroyed and rebuilt with no thought of preserving its character. Thus the architecture that you will encounter for much of the first part of this walk is uninspiring at best. Fortunately, you will see some of the occasional nooks and crannies that still exude the charm of the old Montparnasse.

With the tower to your left, proceed down boulevard du Montparnasse. You will note many restaurants on this part of the street. On the right side of the street, poet James Emanuel lived at No. 55 during the late 1980s; it was here that he wrote his book of poems *Deadly James*. At No. 21, on the corner of boulevard du Montparnasse and rue du Cherche Midi, there was once a cabaret called Mon Village. It featured jazz in 1931.

Turn onto rue du Cherche Midi and go one block to rue Mayet, then turn left. At No. 24 is Tea and Tattered Pages, a used book store and tearoom that has served Americans for many years. Ted Joans has held several readings here.

Retrace your steps to boulevard du Montparnasse and turn right to continue down the street. In 1924, artist Laura Wheeler Waring lodged at a boarding house called Pension Franciana that was once located at No. 11. She won a scholarship from the Pennsylvania Academy of Fine Arts that allowed her to study for one year in Paris.

Directly across the boulevard, behind the beautiful wrought iron doors at No. 20, is the headquarters for the American organization WICE – the Women's Institute for Continuing Education. Photographer Kim Powell-Jaulin held an exhibit here in March 2001, and wine scholar Melba Allen has taught wine appreciation courses here since the 1990s.

Go back to rue du Cherche Midi and cross boulevard du Montparnasse. Then cross rue du Cherche Midi and proceed to rue de Vaugirard. Cross the street and turn right. The first street on the left is the impasse de l'Astrolobe. At No. 3, on the left, sculptor Augusta Savage rented a studio in September 1930. The building is all bricked and shuttered, but one can imagine it once having been an artist's studio. Savage studied for two years at the Grande Chaumière (to be seen later in this walk), and won awards for works that she exhibited at two major art salons in Paris.

As you leave this street, take a peek through the window in the door located across the way at No. 4. Note the courtyard with planters filled with flowers. This is a good example of what may be found behind the heavy doors of buildings in even the most desolate-looking streets of Paris. Retrace your steps to rue de Vaugirard and turn right. Go to the first corner; avenue du Maine is the first street to your right. Turn onto this street and proceed down the right side. From 1921 to 1923, No. 8 was headquarters for the Pan-African Association, a group that sprang from a renewed commitment to Pan-Africanism spearheaded by W. E. B. Du Bois. Historian Rayford W. Logan was one of the officers of this group. A little farther down at No. 14, poet James Emanuel rented an apartment in 1979.

For a taste of old Montparnasse, venture across the street to find No. 21, avenue du Maine. This alleyway, called the *Chemin du Montparnasse* (Montparnasse Way), has been preserved in memory of the artists of the *Ecole de Paris* (the Paris school). They were a lively bunch of foreigners who came to Paris during the first twenty years of the twentieth century and made art history here. The old ateliers, covered by creeping vines, still stand. They are now utilized by artists and the rare shopkeeper. The Montparnasse museum occupies two of these ateliers, and hosts exhibits that recapture the spirit of the area in photographs, paintings, and documents.

Picasso, Chagall, Matisse, Braque, Zadkine, and Léger were among the now famous artists who frequented the Cantine des Artistes (1915-1918), created in this alley by Russian artist Marie Vassilieff. Sculptor Ossip Zadkine not only taught at the Académie de la Grande Chaumière but also had an atelier of his own here, where he instructed students. Among them was Harold Cousins, who was accepted as a student at the atelier in 1949. Ed Clark was another student of Zadkine's, who though primarily interested in painting, decided to try his hand at sculpture while attending the Académie de la Grande Chaumière. Many other African-American artists were influenced by the artists of the *Ecole de Paris*, among them Beauford Delaney, Larry Potter, and Merton Simpson.

Before leaving the *Chemin du Montparnasse* and the avenue

du Maine, look across the street at No. 22. Here stands the Trianon Hotel, where poet Countee Cullen and philanthropist Harold Jackman were guests in the summer of 1928.

Continuing up avenue du Maine, climb the stairs and cross the street to reach place Raoul Dautry. Here you have an unobstructed view of what some consider to be one of the few architectural monstrosities of Paris, the Tour Montparnasse. Enter the square and walk on the right side to pass in front of the Gare Montparnasse (Montparnasse station). This is the third train station to be built on this site, the first two having been outgrown due to the expansion of rail lines to the west and southwest of France. They were subsequently demolished.

W. E. B. Du Bois arrived at the original station in 1918 after he had been dispatched by the NAACP to investigate discrimination against black troops stationed in Paris. James Emanuel was sufficiently impressed by the station and the square that he wrote a poem entitled "Crossing the Square, Montparnasse."

The avenue du Maine continues from the southern point of the square. Follow the sidewalk next to the station to the first large street on the right, rue du Commandant René Mouchotte. Cross the street and walk up the left side. No. 13 on the left is home to Le Petit Journal Montparnasse, a jazz club that opened in 1991. It is the sister club of Le Petit Journal Saint-Michel, located on boulevard Saint-Michel in the 5th *arrondissement*. The neighboring four-star hotel Le Meridien (No. 19) is very popular among American and Japanese travelers. In November 2000, over two hundred African Americans traveling with the Detroit-based social group The Rogues spent an enjoyable week here. Across the street at No. 14 was an apartment building where Chester and Lesley Himes rented a flat during the student revolution of 1968.

Rue du Commandant René Mouchotte ends at the place de Catalogne. On the opposite side of the circle and behind the pillars is rue Vercingétorix. To get there, cross rue du Commandant René

Mouchotte and follow the sidewalk along the circle. Rue du Château is the first intersecting street – look down it for a wonderful view of the Eiffel Tower. Continue around the circle until you reach the pillars and turn right. You will quickly approach a circle of benches punctuated by street lamps and an old church beyond, again reminiscent of the old Montparnasse. This was the approximate site of No. 53, the last address of artist Beauford Delaney before his commitment to Sainte-Anne's hospital and his subsequent death. Delaney was well loved in Paris, and has been described as "gentle" and as "a beautiful man" by those who knew him personally. He was a great friend of James Baldwin. Many people visited Delaney here, including painter Ed Clark and surrealist Ted Joans.

Retrace your steps up rue Vercingétorix and follow place de Catalogne around to the other side of rue Vercingétorix, which runs quickly into rue Jean Zay. This street intersects avenue du Maine. Walk down rue Jean Zay to rue de l'Ouest, cross it to the right, then cross the avenue and enter rue Froidevaux. This street runs next to the wall of the Cimetière Montparnasse, a favorite place of Countee Cullen. It is the burial ground for a couple of the artists of the *Ecole de Paris*. If the entrance near the corner is open, step in and look around for a moment. The circular building that towers over the graves is the Tour de Moulin, the remains of a windmill that used to grind corn during the seventeenth and eighteenth centuries. If you are interested in exploring the cemetery, plan to come back for an extended visit. Free maps are available at the guardhouse next to the entrance. The main entrance is located on boulevard Edgar Quinet.

Going back to rue Froidevaux, turn left and walk up the street to rue Auguste Mie. Turn right onto this street and then left onto rue Cels. The offices of *La Revue Noire* are located at No. 8. This magazine features contemporary black art, be it from Africa, the Caribbean, the US, or elsewhere in the world. It also publishes a literary supplement. All forms of art are incorporated, from sculpture to photography. Long-time Paris resident Hart Leroy Bibbs was featured as part of a group of photographers who captured scenes of Africa that were reproduced in the third edition of the magazine, published in September 1991. Four additional African-American photographers were featured in this issue as well.

Rue Cels ends at rue Fermat. Turn left onto this street. Here, looking over the cemetery wall, you have a view of the distant buildings of Montparnasse. Follow the street back to rue Froidevaux, then turn left. At the avenue du Maine, turn right, proceed to rue de la Gaité, and turn onto this street. It is filled with theaters and sex shops, both reflecting activities that have thrived here since the beginning of the nineteenth century. Historically, the construction of dance halls, theaters, *guinguettes* (outdoor taverns), and upscale restaurants along this minor thoroughfare was driven in part by the business owners' ability to sell wine cheaply outside the city walls. In 1840, the first Montparnasse train station connected the area with the poor countryside of Brittany. The trains also brought poor country girls to the area, which contributed to the establishment of the sex trade here.

At No. 24, on the left, is the Théâtre de la Gaité Montparnasse, where Slide Hampton and other jazz musicians often performed during the 1940s. Nearby is No. 20, the Bobino Music Hall. The current structure bears no resemblance to the theater that stood when Josephine Baker gave her last performance there. The show was literally her last; after performing several days for wildly appreciative audiences, she suffered a stroke and died the following day (Plate 4). Vibraphonist Lionel Hampton is among the African Americans to have performed here after the renovation of the site and its 1986 reopening.

Farther up the street on the left is the rue du Maine. During the late 1920s, Henry Miller lived at the Hôtel Central at No. 1 bis. He was a frequent customer at the high class brothel called the Sphinx, located at No. 31 on the neighboring boulevard Edgar Quinet, and paid for its services by writing pamphlets for the management. Miller was quite impressed by the art and persona of Beauford Delaney; in 1945 he published a moving tribute entitled "The Amazing and Invariable Beauford Delaney" as a return favor for the portrait that Delaney painted of Miller.

Almost directly across rue de la Gaité is the impasse de la Gaité. Crossing rue de la Gaité and entering this street, you will see the building at No. 4 where writer Davida Kilgore had a studio apartment in 1989. She used it as a back drop for her first novel.

Go back to rue de la Gaité and turn right. At the first intersection is boulevard Edgar Quinet, the street where the Sphinx, the first institutionalized bordello on the Left Bank, once operated. This is a market street, and if you venture by on a Wednesday or Saturday morning, you will be able to enjoy the spectacle of neighborhood dwellers shopping for produce, meats and poultry, and even flowers. On Sundays, an arts and crafts fair is held here all day.

Turn left onto boulevard Edgar Quinet and walk to the first intersection, which is rue Poinset. Here you find the place Josephine Baker, which the city of Paris dedicated to her on February 2, 2001. This site was chosen for its proximity to the Bobino Theater where Baker gave her last performance.

Retrace your steps to the corner of boulevard Edgar Quinet and rue de la Gaité. Cross boulevard Edgar Quinet to enter rue du Montparnasse. Note that there are several *créperies* at this end of the street; their presence bears witness to the heavy Breton influence in the development of the area. No. 56 is where the Hôtel Unic stands. Frank Van Bracken, a correspondent for *Ebony* magazine, lived here during the 1950s. No. 42 is still home to the Falstaff Bar, one of the favorites of "the Lost Generation" and visitors from the Harlem Renaissance.

Cross boulevard du Montparnasse and turn right. Walk past the church and turn left onto rue Stanislas. No. 14 is the site of the hotel Résidence Montparnasse. Sociologist Horace Cayton stayed here on a trip during which he intended to research information for a biography of Richard Wright. He was occupying a room here in January 1970, when he died.

Continue up rue Stanislas to boulevard Raspail and turn right.

Follow the boulevard to rue Vavin, and turn left. No. 33 on the corner was once the site of La Boule Blanche, a popular night spot that was frequented primarily by West Indians. It was similar to Le Bal Nègre, a more famous spot located in the 15th *arrondissement*, where African Americans were exposed to the rhythms and dances of the Caribbean. In both cabarets, a dance called *La Biguine* was king.

Turn left onto boulevard Raspail and follow it to the next intersection. This lively little street is rue Bréa. At No. 15 on this street was another apartment occupied by Laura Wheeler Waring. Waring was one of twelve African-American artists who came to Paris to study between 1922 and 1934. These and several other African Americans, including writer Claude McKay, made up what was dubbed the "Negro Colony" of Montparnasse.

Continue down rue Bréa until it intersects with rue Notre-Dame-des-Champs, then turn right. The next street that you will encounter is rue Jules Chaplain. At an unknown number on this street, painter Herbert Gentry and his wife Honey opened a combination art gallery and jazz club in 1947 called Chez Honey. African-American art was featured by day and African-American music was featured by night. Many great artists performed here, including Duke Ellington and Lena Horne. No. 6 on this street was the Maison Watteau, occupied in 1920 by a group of Scandinavian artists who held expositions and taught courses. During the late 1920s, artists Hale Woodruff, Aaron Douglas, and Augusta Savage were students of the Académie Scandinave, presumably located at the same address.

Continue walking down the right side of rue Notre-Dame-des-Champs. No. 70 was once the residence and studio of the great Henry O. Tanner. He and his family lived here from 1904 to 1922. Tanner first came to Paris in 1891 on his way to Rome, but fell in love with the city and made it his home. You may see where he first lived in Paris if you take the Musée d'Orsay walk described in this book.

Proceed to the next intersection, rue de la Grande Chaumière. Turn onto this street. No. 4 was the home of surrealist poet Ted

Joans and his Belgian girlfriend. No. 8 was the home of Nina Hamnett, a British painter who was a friend of writer Claude McKay. McKay reportedly visited Hamnett often here. At No. 10 stood the Académie Colarossi, one of two avant-garde art schools that attracted large numbers of African Americans over the past century. The Académie de la Grande Chaumière at No. 14 displays the names of its foremost professors on plaques affixed to its facade. This school was even more popular than the Académie Colarossi among African Americans. Meta Vaux Warrick Fuller, William Edouard Scott, Loïs Mailou Jones, Ed Clark, and Herbert Gentry are among the African Americans who studied at these two institutions after 1900.

Walk up the street to boulevard du Montparnasse and turn left. Go to the next block which is rue Chevreuse. On the corner, where a large brasserie now stands, the famous Jockey Club once operated. This was the second site for the club, which represented Montparnasse's first night club. You will see the original location later on this tour. Turn onto rue Chevreuse. The American University Women's Club and the American Art Students Club for Women, once located at No. 4, had the dubious distinction of having refused lodging to Meta Vaux Warwick Fuller in October 1899 because she was black. The Women's Club is now known as Reid Hall.

Walk to the corner of rue Chevreuse and rue Notre-Dame-des-Champs and turn right. Continue up the street, passing No. 86 on the right. This was the home of Whistler, the American painter. Artist William H. Johnson, who lived in France from 1926 to 1929, occupied an apartment in this building in 1926. Fernand Léger of the *Ecole de Paris* had a studio in this same building. Students benefiting from the GI Bill could study at his Académie as well as the schools that you have just seen; John Wilson and Richard Boggers were among his pupils. Continue to avenue de l'Observatoire and turn right. On the corner is the famous café La Closerie des Lilas. This is the place from where the original call to writers and artists went out in the early twentieth century, transforming Montparnasse into an international creative arts center for decades. In the post-World War II years, Herbert Gentry commented on the US influence in the area, saying "It was the Americans who made Montparnasse."

Standing on the corner of boulevard du Montparnasse and avenue de l'Observatoire, look across the street to the Port Royal RER station. On this side of the avenue once stood a club called Le Bal Bullier. Its address, 31, avenue de l'Observatoire, no longer exists. It was at the Bal Bullier that boxer Arthur Craven likely met former heavyweight champion of the world Jack Johnson. The two would subsequently meet in the ring in Barcelona, where in 1916, Johnson would knock out Craven in the first round. The Bal Bullier was a hangout for Martinicans in the 1900s, and began to feature jazz during the 1920s. The brasserie that stands on boulevard du Montparnasse and directly opposite the Closerie de Lilas has adopted the name of the old club.

Cross boulevard du Montparnasse and turn right. Walk down the street to rue Campagne Première. On the west corner of rue Campagne Première and boulevard du Montparnasse was the original site of the Jockey Club.. This night spot, which operated from 1923-1930, catered to everyone without distinction of class or wealth. In 1929, it was depicted in the oil painting *The Jockey Club,* by Archibald Motley, which is currently located at the Schomburg Center for Research in Black Culture in New York City. At an unknown number on this street, Claude McKay worked in artist André Lhote's poorly heated studio in 1923; as a result, he caught pneumonia. Turn left and walk up the street on the left side. At No. 9 is a former artists' residence created from materials salvaged from the buildings of the 1889 Paris World Fair. Loïs Mailou Jones had a magnificent studio here.

Jones may be the most celebrated female African-American artist of her time. She first came to Paris to study in 1937, arriving a few months after the death of Henry O. Tanner. Meta Vaux Warwick Fuller was one of her mentors; she played a large part in Jones's decision to come to Paris. Jones took up residence on rue Campagne Première when she studied at the Académie Julian, which can be seen on another walk in this book.

Retrace your steps to boulevard du Montparnasse, turn left and proceed to rue Léopold Robert. Turn onto this street, the left side of which is lined with charming little restaurants, and go to boulevard Raspail. Cross the street and turn right. The Hôtel Le Royal still stands at No. 212; it is the place where Chester Himes would stay when he visited Paris after having moved to Spain in 1970.

Proceed down boulevard Raspail to the large intersection which is place Pablo Picasso. Formerly known as the Carrefour Vavin, it is the cradle of Montparnasse, the place where students from the Latin Quarter used to hangout in the early eighteenth century. Turn onto rue Delambre, the first street on your left that intersects the place.

No. 4 on the right, now the fish market for the illustrious café Le Dôme, was once the address for The Black Manikin, a small publishing house and bookstore that operated during the 1920s and 30s. Run by Edward W. Titus, it published the works of Countee Cullen and Claude McKay. After it closed, an American restaurant called "La Petite Casserole" operated here for a while. Farther down the street at No. 15, on the left, is the Hôtel Lenox, formerly the Hôtel des Ecoles. Man Ray's studio was located here. Abstract painters Ed Clark and Beauford Delaney both stayed in this hotel as well, with Ed Clark later moving across the street to a top floor apartment at No. 22.

Retrace your steps to boulevard du Montparnasse, where you will now see the cafés that made the area truly famous. On the corner at your left is No. 108 – Le Dôme. Claude McKay and his friend Nina Hamnett frequented this place in the 1920s; Albert Alexander Smith, a member of the previously mentioned Negro Colony, worked here during the 1930s; and Ed Clark and Beauford Delaney sold some of Delaney's paintings here in 1956. Le Dôme was extensively renovated in 1923; its beautiful terrace was added at that time.

Down the street on the same side is No. 102 – La Coupole. Of the four cafés on the Carrefour Vavin, this one attracts the most tourists. Josephine Baker was present at the opening of the café in 1927. Langston Hughes and Herbert Gentry were frequent patrons as well. The café was rebuilt in 1989, but it retains the original interior decor. Fernand Léger was one of the artists responsible for the paintings that grace La Coupole's walls and pillars.

Across the boulevard at No. 99 is Le Sélect. After World War II, this was more of an "everyman's café," while La Coupole and Le Dôme were a bit more upscale. It was here where Chester Himes wrote his novel *A Jealous Man Can't Win* and Ed Clark made the acquaintance of *Le Monde* journalist Michel Conil-Lacoste, who favorably reviewed his work and was instrumental in getting Clark a one-man exhibition at the Galerie Creuze. David, the main character of James Baldwin's *Giovanni's Room*, goes to Le Sélect to drink after deserting the Closerie des Lilas.

Up the street from Le Sélect and back at the Carrefour Vavin is the fourth café – La Rotonde – at No. 105. It was the first of the cafés founded at this intersection, and apparently was not as popular among African Americans as the other three. Still, it played a fundamental role in the establishment of the artistic atmosphere of the area, and serves as the anchor of the Carrefour that we know today.

This marks the end of the tour. The nearest metro station is Vavin, located on the corner just in front of the Rotonde.

Paris Reflections
Your Thoughts on the Montparnasse Walk

Notre-Dame-de-Lorette / Opéra Walk

This walk concentrates primarily on the era between the two World Wars, when the area called Pigalle teemed with African-American life. This was particularly true "after hours," for many nightclubs were established by and for American blacks who had come to Paris to seek refuge from the racism of home. Jazz was the new rage in town, and blackness was fashionable. Thus Pigalle was suddenly "the place to be" for many Parisians, white Americans of the "Lost Generation," and a large number of international visitors. On this walk you will see where the heart of Black Paris beat from the late 1910s until around the Great Depression.

We begin at the metro Notre-Dame-de-Lorette, which is adjacent to the church of the same name (Map 6). This quarter of the 9th *arrondissement* is known as Saint-Georges, and its history began during the nineteenth century when the bourgeoisie from neighboring Faubourg Poissonière moved westward to escape the mounting population inhabiting the area. Alexandre Dumas *père* delighted in this quarter and its various architectural styles, saying that it seemed "to have been built with a fairy's wand."

Exit the metro station at rue Bourdaloue and walk to its intersection with rue Chateaudun. Turn left at the corner to walk in front of the church, Notre-Dame-de-Lorette. Built to provide the growing population of the neighborhood with a place to worship, its name was quickly ascribed to the many women of questionable virtue who flocked to the quarter in search of a wealthy husband.

Walk past the church to rue Fléchier, turn left and proceed to the next intersection. The street immediately ahead is rue des Martyrs; enter it by making your way around this awkward intersection. Proceed up the street on the right side. No. 12, now a bank, was once the site of a club called Frisco's. Jocelyn "Frisco" Augustus Bingham, a good friend of Ada "Bricktop" Smith and Josephine Baker, had another very popular club on rue Fromentin (also in the 9th *arrondissement*). In the late 1920s, Bricktop (Plate 5) and Baker opened Frisco's at this address on behalf of their friend.

Continue up the street, noting the many produce stands, butchers, and other food vendors along the way. At rue Manuel, turn right and walk to No. 7 on the right side. This was the first address of Haynes' Restaurant, the oldest African-American eating establishment in Paris. Leroy Haynes, a Kentucky-born GI of World War II, came to Paris in 1949. He married a French woman named Gabby and they opened the restaurant together. Haynes left this address in 1960 when he and Gabby divorced; Gabby remained in the restaurant business at this location and renamed her restaurant "Gabby's." In 1964, Haynes opened a new establishment on rue Clauzel, which you will see in just a few minutes.

Retrace your steps to rue des Martyrs and turn right. Just a few yards away on the opposite side of the street is rue Clauzel. Turn onto this street and walk to No. 3 on the left. Here is Haynes' Restaurant, an icon of African-American history in Paris. Haynes himself was an attraction to the restaurant, due to his size and his larger-than-life personality. But his food drew people in as well. The restaurant's walls are lined with photographs of celebrities, both black and white, who have frequented this place over the years. Haynes died in 1986 but his Portuguese widow, Maria, continues to run the restaurant and frequently holds cultural events here that are relevant to African Americans.

Retrace your steps to rue des Martyrs and turn left. At the next intersection is rue Navarin. Turn left and walk to No. 12 on the right side of the street. Now a public housing residence, this was Eugene Bullard's address from 1920 to 1923. The first African-American combat pilot, Bullard fought for the French Foreign Legion during World War I. As the owner and/or manager of many nightclubs in Pigalle, he was instrumental in the success of "Black Montmartre" during the crazy years after the war. The most important club that he owned was Le Grand Duc, the location of which you will see a little later in this walk.

Once again, retrace your steps to rue des Martyrs and turn left. The next street that intersects on the left is rue Victor Massé. Turn left onto this street and proceed to No. 12 on the right. This was the home of a man named Morris, who owned an extensive collection of African art. Knowing of Alain Locke's interest in African art, Langston Hughes informed him of this collection. In 1885, No. 12 was the address of the infamous cabaret Le Chat Noir; Toulouse-Lautrec immortalized both the tavern and its host, Aristide Bruant, in his whimsical posters. A plaque on the facade of the building commemorates this cabaret. Farther up the street at No. 23 is where blues singer Alberta Hunter lived in 1927. Hunter toured England and continental Europe during that year, singing blues and jazz.

Continue up rue Victor Massé to the next intersection. On the right side of the street is a private alley, flanked on the left by a curved building, the now-defunct Round Theater, with a beautiful blue stained-glass window. The private street is the avenue Frochet; Alexandre Dumas *père* and other renowned French writers and artists once lived on this tiny thoroughfare.

On the left at this intersection is rue Henri Monnier. The chorus girls of *La Revue Nègre* occupied a residence on this street, and Josephine Baker stayed among them for a time.

The street that enters this intersection just to the left of the Round Theater is the rue Frochot. Turn onto this street and walk up to place Pigalle. Once the lively gathering place for Impressionist painters and their writer friends (particularly No. 9, formerly the site of the café

Nouvelle Athènes), part of the square is now sadly desolate. In one of the buildings here, a cabaret called Le Rat Mort was the scene of a racial incident in 1927. It involved an attack by a Cuban man on several black customers. He was taken into custody and sent to jail by a French West Indian who presided over the tribunal of the 18th *arrondissement.*

You are now on the edge of the area known as Pigalle. Rue Pigalle is the street immediately to the left of rue Frochot. Turn onto it and walk a few feet to see No. 66 on the left, which is now a defunct club called The New Moon. This was formerly the Monico, a nightspot owned by Bricktop from 1931 to 1936. Mabel Mercer was her star performer. Across the street (exact address unknown) was once a place called Madame Ericka's Restaurant. Bricktop went to work there after she closed the Monico, and was responsible for booking the entertainment for the restaurant.

Continue down rue Pigalle to No. 59. At this location, the club called Caprice Viennois featured boxer "Panama" Al Brown as singer and bandleader in 1937. No. 55 is the Hôtel de Paris (now a Kyriod hotel), another abode for singer Alberta Hunter. And No. 52 was the site of Le Grand Duc, the famous nightspot that Eugene ("Gene") Bullard opened in 1924. Though Bullard gave Bricktop (so named because of her red hair) her first performing job in Paris, he soon found himself in head-to-head competition with her when she opened her own club just a short block away. Langston Hughes became a dishwasher at the Duc, thanks to the assistance of his friend Rayford Logan. Looking to the north from the little square in front of No. 52, note the partial view of beautiful Sacré-Cœur Basilica.

At the next corner, rue Pigalle intersects three streets, one of which is rue Fontaine. Enter this street and stop to look at No. 1 on the left side. This was where Bricktop's club, called simply "Bricktop's," was located. Having become a successful entertainer at Le Grand Duc, she went on to become legendary once her club was launched. This was largely due to the patronage of Cole Porter and his friends. Bricktop did not discriminate based on the wealth (or lack thereof) of her clientele. She served both common people and royalty in her club, and a good time was had by all. Just opposite at No. 6 was the Cotton Club, a namesake of the club in Harlem; it operated for about a year between 1929 and 1930. Alberta Hunter sang there. No. 5 is now Les Sirènes, but was formerly the site of a bar called l'Escadrille. Owner Eugene Bullard provided a charitable service here in 1940 – he supplied free meals to Americans who were preparing to leave Paris in the face of the Nazi onslaught.

Farther down at No. 16, Zelli's once stood. Owned by an Italian of the same name, it was an extravagant success due to Gene Bullard's talent for management. Bullard worked here before opening Le Grand Duc. Artist Albert Alexander Smith worked at Zelli's as a jazz musician. At the end of the block on the right is No. 24. Now the Pandora Station Café, it was once the Café Lizeux. Jazz musicians often came here. Upstairs was the Hôtel Lizeux, which was an Ethiopian-run establishment when Langston Hughes stayed here in 1937.

Crossing the intersection, continue up rue Fontaine. On the corner at No. 26, Bricktop once again tried her luck at managing a club in 1950. But the magic of the crazy years was gone, and she only managed to stay open until Christmas. R. D. Miller had a tailoring business at No. 31. In 1926, Josephine Baker opened Chez Josephine, a cabaret and restaurant, at No. 40. This was her first club; another would be located off of the Champs-Elysées. No. 42 was the residence of André Breton, a close friend of surrealist poet Ted Joans. Joans often visited the famous French poet here.

Continue to the end of rue Fontaine to place Blanche. Across boulevard de Clichy you have an excellent view of Le Moulin Rouge. A depiction of this cabaret was captured on canvas by Loïs Mailou Jones in 1955; the painting *Le Moulin Rouge* is part of the artist's personal collection. Many African Americans have performed here, from Lew Leslie's Blackbirds in 1929 to Mabel Mercer in 1937 to

Ray Charles and Ella Fitzgerald in 1988. Charles and Fitzgerald performed at the 100th anniversary celebration of the club.

Turn onto rue Blanche, the next street to your left. As you proceed down the street, the second intersection on the left will be with rue Mansart. Turn briefly onto this street to see the nondescript No. 15, where Eugene Bullard once operated an athletic club. Louis Armstrong was a customer here in 1934 and 1935.

Retrace your steps to rue Blanche and turn left. Proceed to No. 61, which is on the right side of the street. This was the site of Chez Florence, owned by Palmer and Florence Embry Jones. Chez Florence was the hottest nightclub in Montmartre for a long while. It was Palmer Jones who suggested to Gene Bullard that he hire Bricktop to entertain at Le Grand Duc, and it was Bricktop who took over Chez Florence and renamed it The Music Box once the Joneses left Paris. This is the site where Sidney Bechet had a gunfight with his banjo player, Mike McKendrick. There were no casualties, but three innocent bystanders were wounded. Bechet was sentenced to fifteen months in prison for the deed; he served eleven of these months and was then deported. He moved to Berlin for a while, then returned to the United States.

Continuing down rue Blanche, the next intersection on the left is rue Chaptal. Turn onto this street. Charles Delaunay and Hughes Parnassié, two French men who loved jazz, founded the Hot Club de France at No. 14. Duke Ellington performed here in 1939 as part of the inauguration of the club, which was conceived to promote jazz as an art form. Offices of the magazine *Jazz Hot*, created by Parnassié, once were at this site as well. Panassié was such a fervent supporter of jazz that he continued to play the forbidden music on his radio station during the Nazi Occupation, translating the titles of the songs into French so that the Germans would not recognize them. Delaunay was responsible for bringing Bill Coleman back to Paris in 1948 and reintroducing Sidney Bechet to Paris in 1949. He was also responsible for organizing the first International Paris Jazz Festival in 1949.

Just next door at No. 16 is the Musée de la Vie Romantique, where the memorabilia of George Sand are housed. You may wish to take a look at the exterior of the museum and its courtyard at the end of the alleyway – here you will be transported back to the nineteenth century.

Continue down rue Chaptal to its intersection with rue Pigalle. You are now at the same intersection where Bricktop and Bullard reigned as queen and king of the nightclubs in Black Montmartre. Turn right onto rue Pigalle and proceed down the street. At No. 36, Bricktop met her future husband Peter Ducongé, and took up residence with him here. Across the street at No. 35, Louis Mitchell of Jazz Kings fame opened Mitchell's American Restaurant. At the intersection with rue La Bruyère, one of the corners was home to The Flea Pit, a place where black musicians and others congregated. It was a favorite hangout for Langston Hughes in 1924.

Rue Pigalle intersects rue Blanche at its southernmost end. Turn right onto rue Blanche and proceed the short distance up the street to the fire station on the right. Across the street, No. 15 is still home to the Théâtre de Paris, where in 1948 Katherine Dunham produced a black ballet called *Le Tumulte Noir*. The musical *Bubbling Brown Sugar* played here thirty years later, and James Emanuel was among the audience for one of the performances.

Before leaving rue Blanche, note that vines have been extended above the ironwork of the gates of the fire station as well as above the garage doors. These are grape vines that are harvested each year by the firemen to make their own wine!

Retrace your steps to the corner, cross the street to the right, and enter rue de la Trinité. This street takes you behind the Sainte-Trinité church. You will see the front of the church momentarily.

Rue de Clichy is at the end of rue de la Trinité; cross it, turn right, and proceed up the street. Looking at the right side of the street, stop in front of No. 16, the Casino de Paris. It is said that the first jazz concert ever to be performed in Paris was held here in 1917, and that Louis Mitchell's Jazz Kings were the musicians who made history in doing so. Josephine Baker also performed here in 1930, after having left Paris for several years. It was here that she performed the song *J'ai Deux Amours, Mon Pays et Paris* (I Have Two Loves, My Country and Paris) for the first time. Next door, No. 20 is now a nondescript office building. But it was once the address of the Apollo Theater, where Sidney Bechet played for the first time with Will Marion Cook's orchestra.

Retrace your steps down rue de Clichy and enter the place d'Estienne d'Orves. Cross rue de Londres and then rue Saint-Lazare to stand on the corner of its intersection with rue de Mogador. From this side of the square you can view the Sainte-Trinité church. Once referred to as a "pompous Gothic revival," this church was commissioned at the time that the Baron Haussmann was bulldozing his way through Paris to create the clean, wide avenues and sweeping vistas that we see today. Apparently Haussmann envisioned Gothic churches as the jewels to crown his classical avenues.

Enter rue de Mogador and proceed to No. 25, the Théâtre Mogador. Josephine Baker starred in the film *La Sirène des Tropiques*, for which several scenes were shot in this theater. A gospel music concert featuring Queen Esther Marrow and the Harlem Gospel Singers was held here in 1995. Tony award winner Linda Hopkins and Maxine Weldon performed in *Wild Women Blues*, which was billed as a "unique presentation of blues, gospel and tap dance." The show ran from January 18 through March 4, 2001. Hopkins and Weldon are no strangers to Paris – in 1996 they performed their successful Broadway show *Black and Blue* at the Théâtre de Châtelet. Hopkins also had a long string of musical performances at the Hôtel Meridien.

Continue down the street past the Galeries Lafayette department store to the intersection with boulevard Haussmann. Jewelry designer Coreen Simpson once had an open invitation to photograph the store's fashion shows; this was an honor that bolstered her career as a fashion photographer in 1960s Paris.

Cross boulevard Haussmann, noting the grandiose building

across the square Diaghilev. This is the rear of the Palais Garnier, the opera house that inspired *Phantom of the Opera*. You will learn more about this building later in the tour. Enter rue Scribe and proceed to the next corner, where you will find the American Express office at No. 11. For decades, this office has represented a link to home, whether as a place to pick up mail, to meet visitors just arriving in Paris, or to *rendez-vous* with friends. Jessie Fauset used this office as a backdrop for her 1933 novel *Comedy: American Style*.

Cross rue Auber and note the gigantic hotel that sits on the opposite corner. This is the Grand Hôtel, where W. E. B. Du Bois united Africans and people of African descent for the Pan-African Congress of 1919. The Pan-African movement, which supports the concept that Africans and people of African descent should work together to achieve political and cultural freedom and power, gained momentum at this conference. Fifty-seven delegates representing fifteen countries adopted resolutions intended to advance the liberation of African colonies and establish self-government for all African peoples. Louis Armstrong and Josephine Baker are among many African Americans who have been guests in the hotel.

Continuing down the street, you will see the Hôtel Scribe at No. 1 on the right. Josephine Baker stayed at this hotel when she was performing at the Olympia in 1968.

Turn right onto boulevard des Capucines and proceed to the first intersection. On the building at the corner of boulevard des Capucines and rue Edouard VII, note the plaque and inscription that commemorate the first moving pictures shown here by the Lumière brothers at what was once the Grand Café. Turn right onto rue Edouard VII and walk to the stately place Edouard Vll, the site of the Théâtre Edouard VII-Sacha Guitry. Sidney Bechet performed here nightly in 1949, in a triumphant return to Paris after his imprisonment and deportation in 1929. He would establish permanent residency in Paris the following year.

Retrace your steps to boulevard des Capucines and turn right.

Map 1

CITY OF PARIS

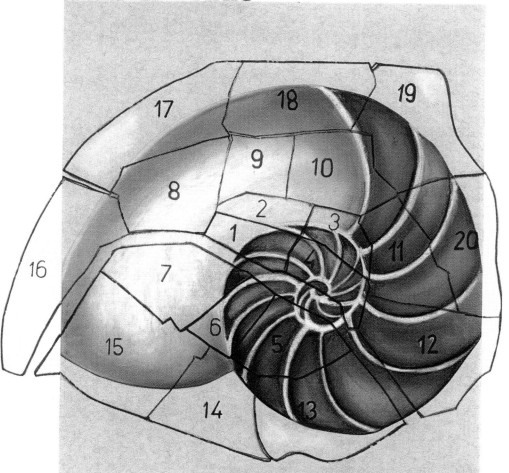

ARRONDISSEMENTS

The 20 arrondissements or districts of Paris unwind from a spiral, with the oldest and

smallest found in the center. The 1st through 4th and the 8th arrondissements are found

on the Right Bank and the 5th through 7th arrondissements are on the Left Bank.

Map 2

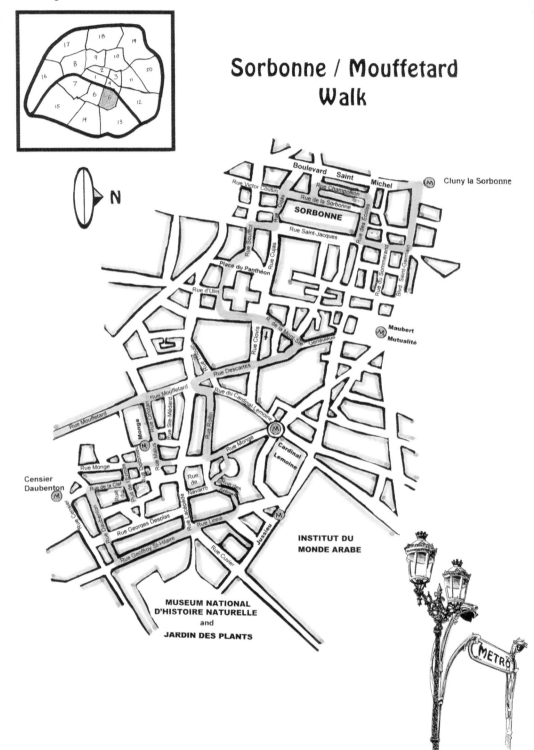

Sorbonne / Mouffetard
Walk

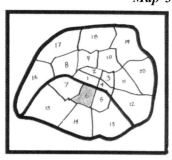

Map 3

Saint-Germain-des-Prés / Luxembourg - A Circular Walk

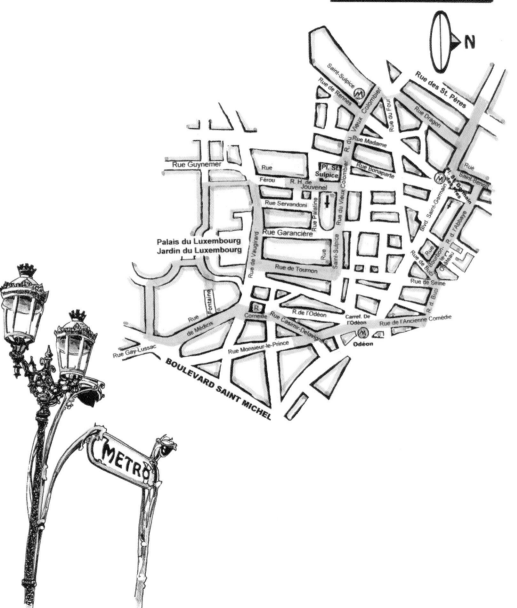

Map 4

Saint-Michel /
Musée d'Orsay Walk

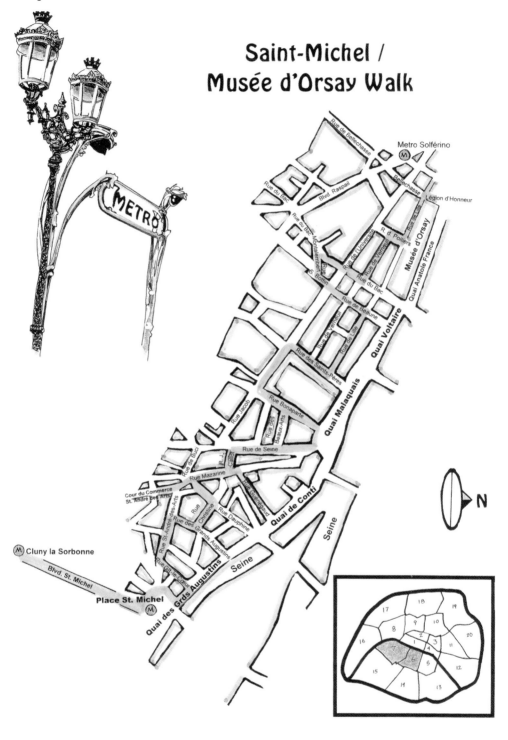

Rue de Bellechasse

Metro Solférino

Rue du Bac

Blvd. Raspail

Bellechasse

Légion d'Honneur

Rue du Bac

R d' Poitiers

Rue de l'Université

Rue de Verneuil

Musée d'Orsay

Rue de Lille

Rue du Bac

Montalembert

S. Bottin

Rue de Beaune

Quai Anatole France

Rue de Verneuil

Rue de Lille

Rue des Saints-Pères

Quai Voltaire

Rue Jacob

Rue Bonaparte

Quai Malaquais

Rue des Beaux-Arts

R. J. Callot

Rue de Seine

Rue de Buci

Rue Mazarine

Cour du Commerce
St. André des Arts

Rue Guénégaud

Quai de Conti

Rue St.-André-des-Arts

Rue Christine

Rue Dauphine

Seine

Rue des Grands Augustins

Rue du Cœur

M Cluny la Sorbonne

Blvd. St. Michel

Quai des Grds Augustins

Seine

Place St. Michel

M

N

17 18 19
8 9 10
16 2 3 20
1 4 11
7 6 5
15 14 13 12

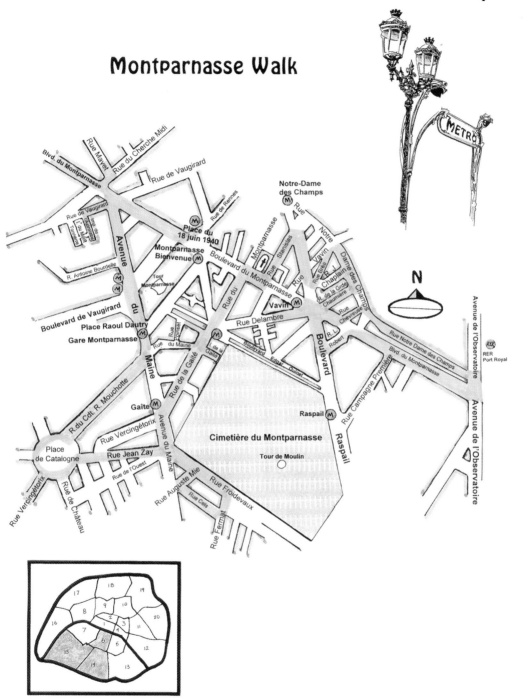

Montparnasse Walk

Map 5

METRO

Rue Mayet

Rue du Cherche Midi

Blvd. du Montparnasse

Rue de Vaugirard

Rue de Vaugirard

Rue de Rennes

Notre-Dame des Champs

Place du 18 juin 1940

Montparnasse Bienvenue

Boulevard du Montparnasse

Rue de Vaugirard

R. Antoine Bourdelle

Tour Montparnasse

Avenue du Maine

Boulevard de Vaugirard

Place Raoul Dautry

Gare Montparnasse

Rue du Maine

Rue du

Rue Delambre

Rue Montparnasse

Rue Stanislas

Rue

Rue Vavin

Rue Huyghens

Chaplain

R. de la Grde Chaumière

Rue Chevreuse

Vavin

Rue Bréa

Notre Dame des Champs

N

Rue Notre Dame des Champs

Avenue de l'Observatoire

RER Port Royal

Avenue de l'Observatoire

R.L. Robert

Boulevard Edgar Quinet

Boulevard

Blvd. du Montparnasse

Rue Campagne Première

Rue de la Gaîté

Gaîté

R. du Cdt. R. Mouchotte

Rue Vercingétorix

Place de Catalogne

Rue Jean Zay

Rue de l'Ouest

Avenue du Maine

Raspail

Raspail

Rue Pointel

Cimetière du Montparnasse

Tour de Moulin

Rue Vercingétorix

Rue de Château

Rue Auguste Mie

Rue Froidevaux

Rue Cels

Rue Fermat

17 18 19

8 9 10 20

16 1 2 3 11

7 4

6 5 12

15 14 13

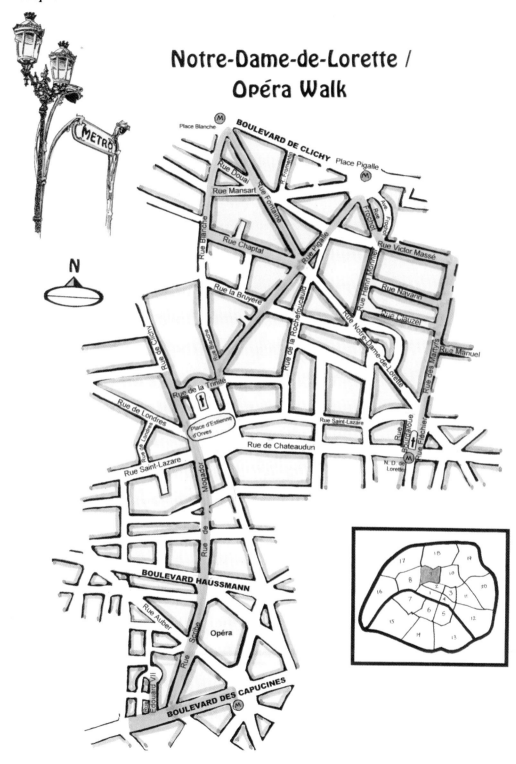

Map 6

Notre-Dame-de-Lorette / Opéra Walk

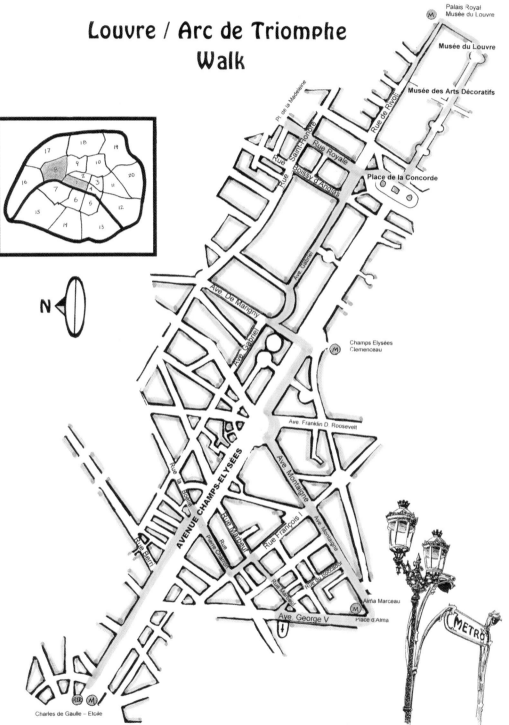

Louvre / Arc de Triomphe Walk

Map 7

Palais Royal
Musée du Louvre

Musée du Louvre

Musée des Arts Décoratifs

Place de la Concorde

Pl. de la Madeleine

Rue Saint-Honoré

Rue Royale

Rue Boissy d'Anglas

Rue de Rivoli

Ave. Gabriel

Ave. De Marigny

Ave. Gabriel

Champs Elysées
Clemenceau

Ave. Franklin D. Roosevelt

AVENUE CHAMPS-ELYSÉES

Rue la Boétie

Ave. Montaigne

Rue Marbeuf

Rue François I

Ave. Montaigne

Rue Pierre Charron

Rue Marbeuf

Rue du Boccador

Alma Marceau

Rue Bern.

Ave. George V

Place d'Alma

METRO

Charles de Gaulle - Etoile

N

17 18 19
9 10
8
2 20
16 7 1 3 11
6 5 4
15 12
14 13

Map 8

The Louvre was originally a fortress with a central keep created to protect the westernmost wall of Paris. It was made into a museum in 1793 during the French Revolution.

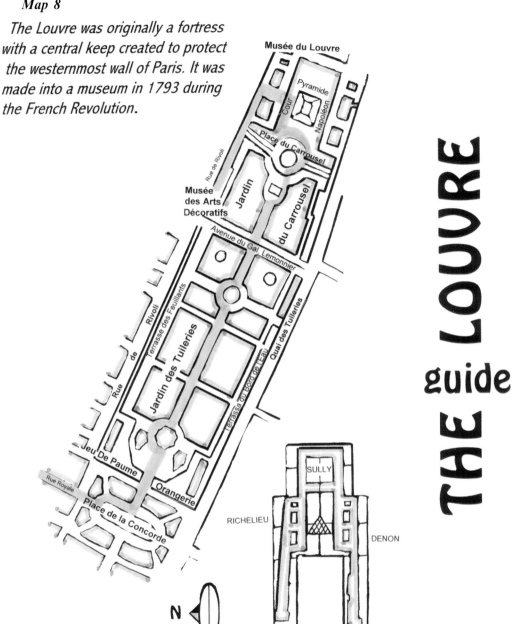

Musée du Louvre

Pyramide

Cour Napoléon

Place du Carrousel

Rue de Rivoli

Musée des Arts Décoratifs

Jardin du Carrousel

Avenue du Gal. Lemonnier

Rivoli

Rue de

Terrasse des Feuillants

Jardin des Tuileries

Quai des Tuileries

Terrasse du Bord de l'Eau

Jeu De Paume

Rue Royale

Orangerie

Place de la Concorde

N

SULLY

RICHELIEU

DENON

THE LOUVRE guide

Plate 1

"Au Nègre Joyeux" in the place de la Contrescarpe

In centuries past, the image of an African or a person of African descent was used on places of business to indicate that chocolate was sold or served there.

Plate 2

*. . . the days when we walked through Les Halles, singing,
loving every inch of France and loving each other . . . .*

James Baldwin, writer

Plate 3

The room was right out of a book and I began to say to myself that dreams do come true and sometimes life makes its own books. Because here I am, living in a Paris garret, writing poems and having champagne for breakfast . . .

Langston Hughes, poet

Plate 4

The funeral of Josephine Baker in Paris

Josephine Baker was honored with a state funeral after her death on April 10, 1975. An estimated 20,000 people crowded around La Madeleine, the church in which the ceremony was held, to bid her farewell.

Plate 5

Singer and nightclub owner Ada Smith, nicknamed "Bricktop."

Plate 6

Tourist in Paris, 1940s

In the sweep of that one vast avenue from the Arch of Triumph to the Louvre through the Elysian Fields – that avenue which kings and emperors have trod and genius and fashion made famous . . . . Before that avenue the streets of the world pale into insignificance.

W. E. B. Du Bois, author, editor, and educator

Plate 7

I'm at last in Paris, city of my dreams. I do manage to see it for myself, the art exhibits, the artists' studios, the sense of leisure, the love of beauty . . . . Will I ever be myself again after all this?

Richard Wright, author

Plate 8

. . . lifting my glance, as with a conscious effort, towards the Orangerie Museum and the hidden Seine River just beyond it, I knew that my thoughts were dropping into the intervening space, into the huge boat basin that had so refreshed my sagging spirit in the autumn of 1968 . . . .

James Emanuel, poet

A short distance away is No. 28, the Olympia Music Hall. The Olympia was founded in 1888 by Joseph Oller, who was also the founder of the Moulin Rouge. Circuses, ballets, operettas, and concerts were held here before the hall succumbed to the competition of the cinema and was transformed into a movie theater. In 1954, it was restored to its original function. All of France's most beloved performers have played here, which has made this a very prestigious hall. Scores of African Americans have performed here as well, among them William Marion Cook, Louis Armstrong, Josephine Baker (as previously mentioned), Sidney Bechet, Mahalia Jackson, Quincy Jones, and Nina Simone.

Retrace your steps up boulevard des Capucines. No. 12 is still the address of the Old England department store, where in 1957 Chester Himes proudly bought "a tan and black checked woolen shirt to go with my brown and black sports jacket and charcoal brown slacks" and "an outrageously expensive pair of English-made yellow brogues" after being paid an advance for the detective novel that he was writing for *La Série Noire*.

Continue up the street to place de l'Opéra. On the corner at No. 3-5 is the Café de la Paix, where many an African American has watched the flow of pedestrians along the boulevard and marveled at the experience of being in Paris. The square is dominated by the Second Empire opera house, the rear of which you saw across the street from Galeries Lafayette. It is called the Palais Garnier (1875), and is named after its architect, Charles Garnier. Though the ostensible purpose of the building was to present opera, the design of the foyer received most of Garnier's attention. His intent was to create a receiving area and staircase that would allow the wealthy to flaunt their clothing and jewelry to the greatest extent possible. It is no wonder that W. E. B. Du Bois was greatly impressed by the grand staircase when he visited in 1899.

Many prominent African Americans have attended performances here. Former slave and abolitionist William Wells Brown was pleased to spot Alexandre Dumas in the crowd when he attended a performance here in 1849. Gwendolyn Bennett and Countee Cullen enjoyed multiple performances here in the mid- to late 1920s. Among the African Americans who have performed here are Leontyne Price, Barbara Hendricks, and Jessye Norman.

This marks the end of the walk. The nearest metro station is Opéra, found in the center of the square.

Paris Reflections
Your Thoughts on the Notre-Dame-de-Lorette / Opéra Walk

Louvre / Arc de Triomphe Walk

The area from the Louvre to the Arc de Triomphe, on the north-west end of the Champs-Elysées, owes its spectacular architecture to the royal family and subsequent leaders of France. Their quest for grandeur and majesty has left us with the wonderful gardens and edifices that we appreciate today. African-American painters, performers, soldiers, and writers (among others) have contributed to the wealth of this area's history (Plate 6). Today's walk will highlight some of their exploits, while taking you past some of the most celebrated monuments of the City of Light.

We begin at the Palais Royal-Louvre metro station (maps 7 and 8). Exit the station at the *Sortie* "place du Palais Royal Côté rue de Rivoli" or "place du Palais Royal / Musée du Louvre." You emerge at the place du Palais Royal, a square that is often filled with young-sters rollerblading, sidewalk artists, and "living" statues. Across rue de Rivoli you see the northernmost section of the Louvre. Cross rue de Rivoli, turn right, and walk to number 107. Here you will find the Musée des Arts Décoratifs, located in the Marsan Pavilion of the Louvre. Though housed in the Louvre, this museum is a separate and distinct institution.

This is one of the few museums in Paris that has exhibited the works of African-American artists. Ed Clark participated in an ex-position of American painters here in 1955. The museum showed Beauford Delaney's work during an exhibit of contemporary painting in 1960. Harold Cousins had the same opportunity to exhibit his sculpture during a similar exposition in 1962. And painter Raymond Saunders participated in a collective exhibit here.

Retrace your steps to the passageway Richelieu (directly opposite the square onto which you emerged from the metro) and turn right to enter. As you walk through the passageway, notice that on your right huge windows afford a view of the splendid Cour Marly. On your left is a view of the Cour Puget. These courtyards have recently been covered with a modern roof to protect the sculptures from the elements.

Emerging into the Cour Napoléon, you immediately encounter the glass pyramids designed by the architectural firm of Chinese-American I. M. Pei. These provide a stark but beautiful contrast to the Old World stateliness of the Louvre, and also allow the public to "remain in touch" with the original architecture while enjoying the modern shopping facilities below ground. Pei's team completed the renovations to the Louvre in two phases, of which the pyramids and the underground shopping area were the first. African-American David Harmon worked on the second phase, the renovation of the Richelieu wing. Harmon was involved in the redesign of the Oriental antiquities and Islamic art rooms of the wing, which encompass over 4000 m² of floor space in the basement and on the ground floor of the museum. The entire renovation project was accomplished in ten years, from 1983-1993. The inauguration of the Richelieu wing took place on the bicentenial of the Louvre's transformation into a museum.

The Louvre was originally a fortress with a central keep created to protect the westernmost wall of Paris. Its conversion into a palace began during the reign of François I (1515-1547); it has been expanded and developed by subsequent monarchs, emperors, and presidents up to the present day. It was made into a museum in 1793 during the French Revolution.

Many African-American artists have studied here: Rex Gorleigh, Archibald Motley, Palmer Hayden, and Hale Woodruff are among them. Most of these artists came alone to sketch and observe the techniques employed by some of the greatest painters of all time. But some also took instruction here and elsewhere – Hayward "Bill" Rivers enrolled at the Ecole du Louvre (Louvre Art School) while Rex Gorleigh studied with painter André Lhote (who would use Claude McKay as a model in his atelier in Montparnasse). One African American – Henry Ossawa Tanner – had his painting *Pilgrims at Emmaüs* displayed here in 1904. In 1991, artist Faith Ringgold utilized the Louvre as a setting for her story quilts entitled *Dancing in the Louvre.*

Leaving the Cour Napoleon, walk under the pastel Arc de Triomphe (not the same as the one at the end of the Champs-Elysées, where this walk ends) into the garden. Here is where the Palais des Tuileries once stood. At the time of William Wells Brown's visit to Paris (1849), the palace still existed and Brown toured its rooms. Once the royal residence of Catherine de Medici, it was destroyed during the uprising known as the Commune of 1871.

After passing the arch, turn left to follow the path to the Porte des Lions. You quickly come to an archway that is flanked by two copper lions, both of which are in an advanced state of oxidation. This leads to the Hall des Lions, part of the Denon wing of the Louvre, where a permanent exhibition of African, Asian, Oceanic, and American (North, Central, and South) art was opened in April 2000. This collection will eventually be moved to the Musée du quai Branly, which will be entirely devoted to primitive art. It is scheduled to open in 2004.

Retrace your steps, turn left and continue down the central path, pausing at the top of the short flight of steps that lead to the gates of the Tuileries Garden. Note the splendid view of the obelisk, the Arc de Triomphe at the far end of the Champs-Elysées, and the highrises of La Défense beyond. Then descend the steps and enter the Tuileries Garden.

Named for tile (*tuiles* in French) factories that were formerly located on this site, the original garden was designed in the Italian style for Catherine de Medici in 1564. Pierre Le Nôtre was chosen for this task. A century later, in 1664, Louis XIV's minister, Colbert, commissioned Le Nôtre's grandson André to refurbish the garden in the French style. William Wells Brown visited this garden at the same time that he toured the palace, and noted the rows of trees that still characterize the grounds today. Brown also remarked on the chairs that were scattered about, describing "hundreds of well-dressed persons . . . sitting on chairs which were kept to let at two sous apiece." Chairs are still found throughout the garden, though the public can now use them at no charge. After a stroll in the garden, James Emanuel was inspired to write the poem entitled "The Boat Basin, Years Later" (Plate 8). As you walk around the circular fountain, look left for a wonderful view of the Musée d'Orsay. Then continue up the central path.

At the far end of the garden you come to a second, octagonal basin. Here you can see two buildings, one to the left and one to the right of the central alley. The building on the right is the Galerie Nationale du Jeu de Paume; artists Hale Woodruff and Clarence Major were both inspired by the Impressionist works that were housed in this museum. The one on the left is the Musée de l'Orangerie. Some Impressionist works are still housed at the Orangerie, but those that were once in the Jeu de Paume are now at the Musée d'Orsay located across the river.

Exit the garden at the gate found between the two museums to enter place de la Concorde. This celebrated square has stood witness to events that are important to both French and African-American history. Most notably, it was the site of over 1,000 executions during the French Revolution's "Reign of Terror." Both King Louis XVI and his queen, Marie-Antoinette, lost their heads here to the guillotine. During this time, the square was called "place de la Révolution," and a statue of a woman who was supposed to represent Liberty was placed here to oversee the grim acts of execution. Both William Wells Brown and journalist Joel Augustus Rogers were inspired by the beauty of the square (well after the Revolution, of course).

African Americans Jessye Norman and Reginald Lewis made history here. Norman was invited to perform for the 200th anniversary of the French Revolution, and sang the French national anthem *La Marseillaise* at the base of the obelisk that stands before you. The fact that Norman was accorded this honor despite not being French created somewhat of a scandal, but her performance thrilled the crowds. Reginald Lewis, the multimillionaire business mogul, was operating from the Hôtel de Crillon located at the northwest corner of the square when he launched his buy-out of the huge French conglomerate TLC Beatrice. Jessye Norman has also been a guest at the Crillon.

Walking to the north side of the square, enter rue Royale. On the left at No. 3 is Maxim's, once a humble restaurant for cabbies who serviced place de la Concorde. It is now part of Pierre Cardin's holdings in the dining and entertainment industry. Richard Wright (Plate 7) was invited to lunch here by photographer and film director Gordon Parks in 1959. Minim's, the less expensive counterpart of Maxim's, is at No. 5. Connoisseurs of crystal, silver, and other luxury items will have a grand time window shopping on this street!

Continue up rue Royale, crossing rue Saint-Honoré and proceed to place de la Madeleine. The huge church, La Madeleine, looks more like a Greek temple thanks to Napoleon Bonaparte. The building began as a church, was commandeered by Bonaparte to create a monument to the glory of the French army, and was reconsecrated with the collapse of the empire. Josephine Baker, who died in Paris in 1975, was given a state funeral here. Twenty thousand people thronged the streets to pay their last respects, as the church itself was filled to capacity.

Cross rue Royale at the corner of place de la Madeleine, looking quickly to the left as you cross to see the harmonious view of the obelisk and the Assemblée Nationale beyond. Retrace your steps to place de la Concorde and turn right. Walking past the Hôtel de Crillon to approach the intersection, observe the large white building across the street. This is the American Embassy, the front of which faces avenue Gabriel. The Embassy, the American Consulate (2, rue Saint-Florentin, 1st *arrondissement*), and the US Ambassador's residence (41, rue Faubourg Saint-Honoré, 8th *arrondissement*) have been the sites for many events relevant to African Americans. Bill Rivers' art was displayed at the Embassy in 1960. In 1963, James Baldwin organized and led a silent march on the Embassy in support of Dr. Martin Luther King Jr.'s March on Washington. In 1999, the Embassy organized a visit for the Reverend Jesse Jackson. Jackson met with African Americans in the private sector and preached at the American Church. Cultural events such as Quincy Jones' receipt of the Legion of Honor, Toni Morrison's reception in honor of her Nobel Prize, and many others have been partly or entirely organized and sponsored by the American government.

Cross rue Boissy d'Anglas and avenue Gabriel to take a look at the front of the Embassy. Then walk up the left side of avenue Gabriel. No. 1 is the theater of the Espace Pierre Cardin, once the home of the club Les Ambassadeurs. A *café-concert* (cabaret) during the Impressionist period, Les Ambassadeurs became one of the most popular nightclubs in Paris. Many African Americans performed here, including Palmer Jones, Florence Mills, Noble Sissle's orchestra (with Sidney Bechet on clarinet), and Dizzy Gillespie. Pierre Cardin purchased the space in 1970. Several jazz concerts were held at the Espace Pierre Cardin in 1978, including a tribute to Duke Ellington given by Cat Anderson and other members of the Duke's orchestra.

Walk up avenue Gabriel, noting the gardens of the Champs-Elysées on your left and the walls protecting the magnificent *hôtels particuliers* (mansions) on your right (the US Ambassador's residence and the British Embassy are among them). The stretch of garden on the left was created by André Le Nôtre beginning in 1670, again at the command of Colbert. The gardens of the mansions on the right originally extended to the border of the Champs-Elysées gardens. Some of the pavillions in Le Nôtre's gardens are now restaurants.

As the street curves to the left, look right to note the wrought iron gate topped by the gilded letters RF and a cock that surveys the Elysée Gardens. This is the rear of the Elysée Palace, the official residence of the French president.

As you approach the intersection of avenue Gabriel with avenue de Marigny, you will note the Marigny Theater across the street. The American Expeditionary Force held a musical performance here in 1917 that featured Louis Mitchell and the Jazz Kings, Noble Sissle, Sidney Bechet, and Arthur Briggs. Josephine Baker also performed here in 1934 and 1935 in the Offenbach opera *La Créole.*

Cross avenue de Marigny, turn left, and proceed to the Champs-Elysées. Stop at the corner to take in the splendor of the view before you. The Grand Palais is the building across the street on the right, while the Petit Palais is the smaller building to the left. In the distance gleams the gilding of Pont Alexandre III and the roof of the Hôtel des Invalides.

Cross the avenue des Champs-Elysées to stand at the corner of place Clemenceau and to get a closer look at the Grand Palais. This building, along with the Petit Palais, was constructed for the Universal Exposition of 1900. Before this time, the site was occupied by the mammoth Palais de l'Industrie that was built for the Universal Exposition of 1855. It was demolished to make way for the Grand and Petit Palais. Both the Palais de l'Industrie and the Grand Palais housed state-sponsored art exhibits, or *salons*, at which prizes were awarded for various works. In 1896, Henry O. Tanner won an honorable mention for his painting *Daniel and the Lion's Den.* He continued to exhibit here until 1924. Many other African Americans have also exhibited at the Grand Palais, including Loïs Mailou Jones, Meta Vaux Warwick Fuller, Ed Clark, and Barbara Chase-Riboud.

Turn right at place Clemenceau and proceed up the Champs-

Elysées. The gardens on this side of the avenue are a bit less sumptuous than those you've just seen, but they are a welcome respite from the concrete that you will find farther up the street. Reaching the Rond-Point (roundabout), stop for a moment to appreciate the magnificent floral patterns that grace the fountains here. Then cross avenue Franklin D. Roosevelt and walk to the next intersection. Turn left to enter avenue Montaigne and proceed down the left side of the street.

Here you have entered a shopper's paradise, as numerous designer boutiques line this street. At the far end of the street, No. 15 on the right is the Théâtre des Champs-Elysées. It was here that the military jazz band of James Reese Europe dazzled the attendees of the Conference of Allied Women in 1918. But even more significant is the fact that Josephine Baker debuted in *La Revue Nègre* at this theater in 1925. This show launched the obsession that Paris experienced for "everything black," reinforcing what had already begun with Picasso's use of African forms for his *Les Demoiselles d'Avignon*.

La Revue Nègre, which also boasted Sidney Bechet in the orchestra and William Marion Cook and his son Mercer as singers, paved the way for many other African Americans to perform here. Louis Armstrong, Katherine Dunham, Barbara Hendricks, the Alvin Ailey Dance Troupe, and Quincy Jones have all graced the theater's stage. Downstairs at the now defunct Club des Champs-Elysées, Lena Horne and the Nicholas Brothers performed as well as Josephine Baker.

Next door to the left of the theater is the Espace Drouot Montaigne. This was where Josephine Baker opened her second club, Chez Josephine, in 1948. (Her first club, also called Chez Josephine, was located in Montmartre.) From December 2000 through February 2001, an exhibit honoring Baker's life was held here. It consisted of posters and illustrations depicting Baker in costume, film clips of her performances, personal effects, gowns from several of her shows, newspaper articles, photographs and much more.

On February 1, 2001, a reception was held at the Drouot to both honor Josephine Baker and to celebrate Black History Month. Ursuline Kairson performed, personal acquaintances of Baker shared their memories of her, and participants viewed the exhibit. Two African-American-owned Paris restaurants, Percy's Place and Bojangles, supplied the *hors d'œuvres* for the event.

Continue down avenue Montaigne until you reach place de l'Alma. Cross avenue Montaigne to stand in front of the Café Francis and the entrance to the Alma-Marceau metro station. Here you have a lovely view of the Eiffel Tower. Near the entrance to the underground expressway is a replica of the torch held by the Statue of Liberty. This place has become a shrine to Princess Diana, as it stands at the mouth of the tunnel in which the accident that claimed her life occurred.

It is believed by many that the idea behind the Statue of Liberty was to commemorate the liberation of slaves in America, and that models for the original statue depicted a black woman. The question has inspired debate that continues in academic circles, the press, and cyberspace. While research on the issue continues, one thing seems clear – the myths surrounding Lady Liberty have become almost as colossal as the statue itself.

From place de l'Alma, turn right onto avenue Georges V and walk up the right side of the street. On the left at No. 23 is the American Cathedral. This was the site of memorial services for Martin Luther King, Jr. (1968) and James Baldwin (1987). Julia Wright held a showing of Madison D. Lacy's film *Richard Wright – Black Boy* here in 1995. And on a joyous note, several concerts featuring gospel music were held at the cathedral during the 1990s. The Crenshaw Gospel Choir of Los Angeles, led by Iris Stevenson, gave a particularly memorable performance in 1994.

Turn right onto rue Boccador just in front of the cathedral, go to the first intersection and turn left onto rue Marbeuf. Walk up the left side of the street to the intersection with rue François I. On the corner is the Hôtel Claridge Bellman, where W. E. B. Du Bois and Paul Robeson were warmly received during the World Peace Conference of 1949.

Turn left onto rue François I and proceed to No. 41. This was once the location of Fashion Fair Cosmetics. Two African-American women, Nicole Johnson (managing director) and Kathleen Dameron (*gérante*, or manager), ran the offices here. During the 1990s, Fashion Fair often supported events held by SISTERS – An Association of African-American Women in France.

Continue down rue François I to rue Pierre Charron and turn right. You are now heading back toward the Champs-Elysées. No. 67 on the left was briefly the home of Chez Sidney, a club owned and operated by the celebrated jazz clarinetist Sidney Bechet. After his Paris debut with *La Revue Nègre*, he became part of the Montmartre scene. Having been imprisoned after a gun battle with fellow band member Mike McKendrick, he was subsequently deported in 1929. He went back to the US where he became an established musician, and returned to Paris in 1949. Because of the exceptional support that his fans displayed at his concerts, he decided to move to Paris permanently. He did so in 1950 and experienced extreme popularity, performing up until his death from lung cancer in 1959.

Cross the Champs-Elysées at the nearest crosswalk to enter rue La Boétie on the opposite side of the avenue. At No. 124 is the Chesterfield Café, the home of the longest-running gospel brunch in Paris. Groups from the United States, the Caribbean, France, and other countries have regaled the Chesterfield's clientele on Sunday afternoons for over five years, and the restaurant is often filled to capacity for these performances.

Retrace your steps to the Champs-Elysées and turn right. Proceed up the street. At No. 92 on the right is the entrance to the Hôtel Langeac. Thomas Jefferson lived here from 1785-1789, when he served as the US Ambassador to France; a plaque to the left of the wrought iron entrance commemorates this. It is here where Sally Hemings resided with Jefferson and was rumored to have conceived his child.

Across the avenue, Fouquet's stands at No. 99 on the corner of avenue Georges V. Cyrus Colter used this café as a backdrop for his 1979 novel *Night Studies*, as did Richard Wright for his unpublished novel *Island of Hallucination*. In the 1960s, *Ebony* magazine had offices on avenue Georges V about one block away from the Champs-Elysées.

Continuing up the avenue, you reach the renowned roundabout at place Charles de Gaulle – Etoile and its centerpiece, the Arc de Triomphe. The Arc lies in a perfect line with the obelisk at place de la Concorde and the Louvre beyond. It was erected by Napoleon Bonaparte in honor of his armies and their conquests. Completed in 1836, it became the resting place for France's unknown soldier in 1921. William Wells Brown climbed to the top of the arch during his 1849 visit, and in 1919, Henry O. Tanner relegated it to canvas in his oil painting entitled *The Arch*. Countee Cullen was inspired to write the poem "At the Etoile" after a visit to the tomb of the unknown soldier in 1929, and aviator Eugene Bullard rekindled the eternal flame here at the request of General Charles de Gaulle in 1954.

As a monument to military victory, the Arc de Triomphe is a symbolic place that has been used by conquering nations to celebrate their prowess. The Prussians and the Nazis both paraded past the arch to celebrate their respective victories over France, and the Allied forces that eventually defeated them did the same. Though the US government did not allow the decorated regiments of black American soldiers to take their rightful place in the Allied march after the victory of World War I, many of the soldiers who passed the arch after the liberation of Paris during World War II were African-American.

Special honors were bestowed upon the Harlem Hellfighters (the 369th infantry regiment) of World War I by the French government. It was during this war that Gene Bullard fought with the French Foreign Legion and was decorated for his military service. In July 1941, Josephine Baker, who was awarded the Cross de Lorraine (symbol of the French Resistance movement of World War II), was photographed in full French uniform with the Arc de Triomphe at her back by the French newspaper *Défense de la France*. To assist in the French war effort, she joined the Auxiliary Corps of the French Air Force. She was awarded the Legion of Honor for her military service. Baker later had the occasion to walk down the avenue with General de Gaulle in a show of solidarity for him during the 1968 uprisings.

We have now reached the end of this walk. The nearest metro station is Charles de Gaulle – Etoile.

Paris Reflections
Your Thoughts on the Louvre / Arc de Triomphe Walk

Profiles –
Black People in Paris Reflections

The following is a list of African Americans, Africans, and people of African descent who are mentioned in the Introduction and walking tours of *Paris Reflections.*

AILEY, ALVIN

Dancer, dance troupe leader. The Alvin Ailey Dancers performed in Paris during the 1960s, and later celebrated their twentieth anniversary by giving a performance at the Théâtre de la Ville at Châtelet.

ALDRIDGE, IRA

Actor. Famed Shakespearean actor Aldridge played Othello in Paris in 1867.

ALI, MUHAMMAD

Musician. Ali, a drummer, was one of many jazz musicians who lived and worked in Paris in the 1960s and 1970s.

ALLEN, MELBA

Enologist. Allen is a longtime Paris resident with a French degree in enology.

ANDERSON, CHRISTIANN

Editor, illustrator, author. Works include *Food for the Soul*, *Paris Reflections* and logo design for Discover Paris! A resident of Paris since 1991, Anderson conceived of *Paris Reflections* to celebrate and honor the history of the many African Americans whose lives and experiences help to illuminate the City of Light.

ANDERSON, MARIAN

Performer. Anderson performed at Saint-Chapelle on the Ile de la Cité in September 1965.

ANDERSON, WILLIAM "CAT"

Musician. Trumpeter Anderson was a member of the famous Duke Ellington Orchestra, and paid tribute to the late Duke in a Paris concert in 1978.

ANGELOU, MAYA

Author, dancer. Works include *I Know Why the Caged Bird Sings* and *Singin' and Swingin' and Gettin' Merry Like Christmas*. Angelou performed in Paris at the Mars Club and the Rose Rouge in 1953 during her successful run in the opera *Porgy and Bess*.

ARMSTRONG, LOUIS

Performer. Trumpet player and singer Armstrong performed several times in Paris during the 1930s, 40s, and 50s. There is a square named after him in the 13th *arrondissement*.

ARNEAUX, J. A.

Actor, publisher. Arneaux studied in Paris in 1876, returned to the United States to a launch a successful career in Shakespearean acting and then in journalism before returning to Paris in 1887.

BAKER, JOSEPHINE

Performer. Baker went to Paris in 1925 with the show *La Revue Nègre* and enjoyed overnight success in her role. She adopted France as her home country, always returning even though her singing and acting career took her all over the world. She died in Paris in 1975.

BALDWIN, JAMES

Author, civil rights activist. Works include *Go Tell It on the Mountain*, *Giovanni's Room*. Baldwin went to Paris in 1948 and stayed for eight years. During this time, he wrote *Go Tell It on the Mountain* and met his friend and lover, Lucien Happersberger. He eventually settled in the French provencial town of Saint-Paul-de-Vence, where he died in 1987.

BEARDEN, ROMARE

Artist. Bearden was part of the African-American artists colony that was centered in Paris after World War II. He exhibited his work in Paris during the 1940s and 50s.

BEATTY, ARTHUR

Artist. Beatty exhibited his works in various Paris galleries during the early 1980s.

BECHET, SIDNEY

Musician. Adored by the French, Bechet was a clarinetist and saxaphonist whose fame paralleled that of Josephine Baker. He debuted in Paris in 1920, appeared with Baker in the show *La Revue Nègre* in 1925, left the city in 1929 after serving a prison term for shooting a fellow musician, and returned definitively in 1950. He died in a small town outside of Paris in 1959.

BENNETT, GWENDOLYN

Author, poet, educator. Bennett spent a year in Paris as a young single woman in the 1920s, and was inspired to write short stories based upon her impressions and experiences during that time.

BIBBS, HART LEROY

Photographer. A resident of Paris for over thirty years, Bibbs specialized in portraits of jazz musicians. Jazz not only inspired his photography, but also his poetry. His jazz portraits were exhibited in many places in Paris.

BINGHAM, JOCELYN "FRISCO" AUGUSTUS

Performer, nightclub manager. Bingham, a friend of Josephine Baker and Bricktop, ran a club called Frisco's during the early 1930s.

BOGGERS, RICHARD

Artist. Boggers came to Paris during the 1950s to study with Fernand Léger.

BRAXTON, ANTHONY

Musician. Braxton, a composer and multi-instrumentalist (piano, clarinet, flute, saxophone), played jazz in Paris in the late 1960s and 1970s.

BRICKTOP (*see* SMITH, ADA)

BRIGGS, ARTHUR

Musician. One of the African Americans who enjoyed professional success as a trumpet player and orchestra leader in Paris during the interwar years. He was interned by the Germans during the Nazi Occupation of Paris during World War II.

BRITTON, SYLVESTER

Artist. Britton went to Paris in 1952. He studied at the Académie de la Grande Chaumière in Montparnasse.

BROWN, AL "PANAMA AL"

Boxer, bandleader, and performer. Al Brown lived in Paris during the 1920s and 30s, experiencing fame, a reversal of fortune, and a renaissance when he reclaimed his bantam-weight championship there in 1938.

BROWN, MARION

Musician. Part of the Free Jazz scene of the 1960s, Brown returned to Paris to give concerts in the 1970s and 80s. His instuments include the flute, clarinet and saxophone.

BROWN, WILLIAM WELLS

Former slave, author, and abolitionist. Brown traveled to Paris for an extensive visit in 1849.

BULLARD, EUGENE "GENE"

Combat pilot, nightclub owner and manager. Bullard was a major player in the night life of Black Paris during the interwar years. He was finally driven from his adopted country by the Nazi invasion of Paris during World War II.

BYAS, DON

Musician. A saxophonist who went to Paris in 1946 with Don Redman's orchestra, Byas eventually made the city his home.

CARMICHAEL, STOKELY

Civil rights activist. Carmichael spoke at the Salle de la Mutualité in 1967 and appeared on French television in 1978.

CAVANAUGH, INEZ

Blues and jazz singer. The late 1940s brought Cavanaugh and her Danish jazz aficionado husband to Paris, where she opened her jazz club and kitchen Chez Inez. She moved back to the United States in 1952.

CAYTON, HORACE

Sociologist. Cayton went to Paris in 1936 to participate in an international conference of writers. He returned three decades later to research information on Richard Wright and died there.

CÉSAIRE, AIMÉ

Founder of the *Négritude* movement. A resident of Martinique, Césaire went to Paris in 1931 to study at an esteemed high school. He was elected to the French National Assembly soon after the end of World War II, and participated in the Congress of Negro Artists and Writers that took place at the Sorbonne in 1956.

CHARLES, RAY

Performer. Charles performed in Paris during the last three decades of the twentieth century, including headlining at the prestigious Olympia Music Hall.

CHASE-RIBOUD, BARBARA

Author, artist. Written works include *Sally Hemings* (novel) and *Portrait of a Nude Woman as Cleopatra* (poetry). Barbara Chase went to Paris in 1961 after finishing a degree in fine arts at Yale University. She made the city her home, met and married photographer Marc Riboud, and established her artistic and literary career in the subsequent years. She now calls Rome home.

CLARK, EDWARD

Artist. One of many artists who went to Paris to study under the GI Bill after World War II, Clark was among the few whose work was exhibited at several galleries in town.

CLARKE, KENNY

Musician. Having wanted to visit France since his preteen years, Clarke saw Paris for the first time in 1937. He went back during World War II, performed there in 1948 and 1949, and moved there permanently in 1956.

COLEMAN, BESSIE

Aviator. Coleman received her pilot's license from the International Aeronautical Federation in Paris in 1921.

COLEMAN, BILL

Musician. Coleman moved to Paris to work as a trumpet player in 1948, and eventually made it his permanent home. He married in Paris in 1953, and became a regular performer at a 5th *arrondissement* jazz club for much of the 1950s.

COLEMAN, WALTER

Artist. A contemporary of Chester Himes, Coleman and his Swedish wife Torun lived in Paris during the 1950s and 60s.

COLEMAN, WILLIAM EMMET

Architect. Yet another African American who went to Paris after World War II to study under the GI Bill, Coleman enrolled at the Sorbonne after having finished a degree at Yale University.

COLTER, CYRUS

Author. Colter's novel *Night Studies* (1979) vividly describes several scenes in Paris.

COOK, MERCER

Educator, foreign ambassador. A frequent visitor to Paris in the 1930s, Cook taught about African-American life in France during his tenure at Howard University. He participated in the Congress of Negro Artists and Writers held at the Sorbonne in 1956.

COOK, WILL MARION

Band leader. Cook's group, the Southern Syncopated Orchestra, was responsible for bringing several jazz musicians to Europe for the first time. Cook's son Mercer, who would eventually grow up to be a college professor, went to Europe with him and performed at the Théatre des Champs-Elysées in *La Revue Nègre* in 1925.

COOPER, ANNA JULIA

Former slave and educator. Cooper studied in Paris before World War I, and returned to enroll at the Sorbonne in 1924. She successfully defended her dissertation in 1925.

COUSINS, HAROLD

Artist. Another beneficiary of the GI Bill, Cousins studied sculpture under Zadkine and went on to successfully exhibit his work at many Paris galleries. He left Paris to go to Brussels in 1967, after having lived in the City of Light for eighteen years.

COUSSEY, ANNE

Love interest of Langston Hughes. Coussey was a student of Raymond Duncan in Paris in 1924 when she met and fell in love with Langston Hughes.

CROWDER, HENRY

Musician, songwriter. As part of the jazz band known as Eddie South's Alabamians, Crowder met and fell in love with Nancy Cunard, a British heiress who lived in Paris. They took up residence together in the late 1920s and stayed together for three years. He worked with Cunard at her publishing company, The Hours Press.

CULLEN, COUNTEE

Poet, author. Works include *The Black Christ* and *The Medea and Other Poems*. Cullen first visited France in 1926, returned in 1928 to pursue his writing, left once again, and subsequently returned several times during the summers of the 1930s.

DAMERON, KATHLEEN

Business manager, consultant in intercultural communication. Dameron was one of two African-American women to manage the offices of Fashion Fair Cosmetics during the 1990s.

DAVIS, ANGELA

Civil rights activist, educator. Davis studied at the Sorbonne during her "junior year abroad" as a matriculate of Brandeis University in 1963 and 1964. She returned to Paris in 1977 to participate in a rally in support of the Wilmington 10.

DAVIS, MILES

Musician. Davis visited Paris many times, the first of which was as a participant in the jazz festival of 1949. Though he loved the city, he never considered moving there.

DELANEY, BEAUFORD

Artist. Delaney was a good friend of James Baldwin, and may have been inspired by Baldwin to move to Paris in 1953. He was quite successful there, exhibiting both portraits and abstract works. He died in Paris in 1973.

DOUGLAS, AARON

Artist. Douglas was a recipient of the Julius Rosenwald scholarship, and traveled to Paris to study. He attended the Académie de la Grande Chaumière and the Académie Scandinave during the interwar years.

DOUGLASS, FREDERICK

Former slave, abolitionist. During a visit to Paris in 1886, Douglass saw among other things, the National Library (where he found his own narrative on file), the site of the Bastille fortress, and the Senate chambers.

DU BOIS, W. E. B.

Educator. Du Bois visited Paris in 1918 to investigate discrimination charges against black troops during World War I, and returned in 1919 to organize and participate in the Pan-African Congress that petitioned the Versailles Peace Conference for the empowerment of colonial Africa.

DUCONGÉ, PETER

Musician. Ducongé was a saxophonist who met and married Bricktop in Paris.

DUMAS, ALEXANDRE *PÈRE*

Playwright and author. Works include *The Three Musketeers* and *The Count of Monte Cristo*. The grandson of a French noble and a black Antillian woman, Dumas was one of the most celebrated playwrights of the nineteenth century. While the French seldom considered his race, he was respected and admired by American blacks as being a person of color.

DUNHAM, KATHERINE

Dancer. Dunham's famous New York troupe of African-American dancers visited Paris in the late 1940s and early 1950s.

ELLINGTON, DUKE

Musician, orchestra leader. Ellington and his band played to very appreciative crowds in Paris in 1933. The Duke's first postwar visit to Paris took place in 1948, when Boris Vian welcomed him to the Club Saint-Germain.

EMANUEL, JAMES

Poet, educator. Emanuel first visited France as a Fulbright scholar in 1968, when he went to the University of Grenoble, then again in 1971 as a Fulbright lecturer at the University of Toulouse. He took up residence in Paris in 1984.

EUROPE, JAMES REESE

Soldier, military band leader. Leader of the brave and successful Harlem Hellfighters, the 369th Infantry Regiment of World War I, Europe's claim to fame in France is his introduction of jazz to various areas of the country during and after the war.

EWELL, DON

Musician. In 1971, Ewell was a featured performer at the now defunct Riverboat jazz club in the 6th *arrondissement*.

FAUSET, JESSIE

Author, educator. A Harlem Renaissance writer, Faucet lived in Paris for several months in 1924 and 1925. Some of her work was published in Paulette Nardal's *Revue du Monde Noir* (Black World Review).

FITZGERALD, ELLA

Singer. Fitzgerald was invited to perform at the 100th anniversary celebration of the Moulin Rouge in 1988.

FRAZIER, E. FRANKLIN

Sociologist, educator. Frazier worked at UNESCO for two years beginning in 1951. He was nominated to be a member of the executive council of the *Société Africaine de Culture* in 1956.

FULLER, META VAUX WARRICK

Artist. Fuller arrived in Paris in 1899. She became well acquainted with Henry O. Tanner and his wife during her stay, and benefited from Tanner's professional guidance. She studied at the Académie Colarossi and also with the master sculptor Auguste Rodin. She returned to the United States in 1902.

GAINES, ERNEST

Author. Works include *The Autobiography of Miss Jane Pittman* and *A Gathering of Old Men*. Gaines was part of the 1992 Sorbonne conference "African Americans and Europe" and was honored by the French in receiving the *Ordre des Arts et des Lettres* during the 1996 Salon du Livre.

GENTRY, HERBERT

Artist. Gentry first saw Paris during the Liberation of 1944. He returned two years later to study at the Ecole des Beaux-Arts and the Académie de la Grande Chaumière. Leaving for the US in 1951, he returned again in 1953. Though he successfully exhibited his work in Paris, he found wider acceptance in the Scandanavian countries of Europe.

GIBSON, RICHARD

Journalist. Gibson is a descendent of Henry O. Tanner. He studied at the Sorbonne on the GI Bill and worked for Agence France Presse in Paris during the 1950s.

GILLESPIE, DIZZY

Musician. In February 1948, Dizzy Gillespie gave the first major bebop jazz concert in Paris. It was a huge success.

GILLIAM, SAM

Artist. Gilliam's work has been especially appreciated by Darthea Speyer, who has exhibited his work in her gallery at least five times since 1970, including a retrospective in 1991.

GORLEIGH, REX

Artist. One of the African-American artists in Paris during the 1930s, Gorleigh spent much of his time studying on his own at the Louvre.

GORDON, DEXTER

Musician. Gordon's name is inextricably linked with Paris due to his role in the movie *Round Midnight,* filmed there in 1986.

GROSVENOR, VERTAMAE

Poet, actress, author. Grosvenor went to Paris in 1958, where she rented a room on rue de Fleurus, the same street on which Gertrude Stein and Alice B. Toklas lived. Enamored of the city during her first visit, she was much less so during her second visit ten years later. She was one of the African Americans who helped the students during their uprising in May 1968.

HAMPTON, LIONEL

Musician. Hampton, a drummer and vibraphonist, performed in Paris during the 1950s and 60s at places such as the Ringside club and the Living Room.

HAMPTON, SLIDE

Musician. A jazz trombonist, Hampton performed in Paris periodically from the 1940s to the 1970s.

HARMON, DAVID

Architect. Harmon worked with a team of architects and other professionals on Phase II of the renovation of the Louvre beginning in 1993. He was responsible for the rooms housing Islamic art and Oriental antiquities.

HARRINGTON, OLIVER

Cartoonist. A good friend of Richard Wright and Chester Himes, Harrington lived in Paris during the heyday of African-American intellectuals on the Left Bank in the 1950s.

HAYDEN, PALMER

Artist. Hayden, along with Hale Woodruff, traveled to Paris in 1926 using funds provided by the Harmon Foundation. He was part of the "Negro Colony" of Paris during the 1920s and 1930s.

HAYNES, LEROY

Actor, restaurateur. Haynes' Paris career spanned the years from 1949 to 1986. He was the creator of Haynes' Restaurant, a culinary institution that exists to this day on rue Clauzel in the 9th *arrondissement*.

HEATH, GORDON

Performer. Heath made Paris his home in 1948. He owned and performed at the nightclub Club de l'Abbaye in the Saint-Germain area.

HEMINGS, SALLY

Slave of Thomas Jefferson. Hemings lived with Jefferson during his tenure as US Ambassador to France during the years 1785-1789.

HENDRICKS, BARBARA

Singer. Hendricks made her Paris opera debut in 1982, playing Juliette in *Romeo and Juliette.* She has been awarded both the Legion of Honor and the *Commandeur des Arts et des Lettres* by the French government.

HIMES, CHESTER

Author. Works include *A Rage in Harlem* and *The Crazy Kill.* Himes set sail for Paris in 1953, and spent the remainder of his life in France and other European countries. His book *The Five-Cornered Square* won the literary prize *Le Grand Prix du Roman Policier* in France in 1958 and Himes was offered a contract to write his detective stories as a result. These were the source of his acclaim in France.

HOLIDAY, BILLIE

Singer. Holiday was a featured artist in 1958 at the former jazz club La Rose Rouge.

HOPKINS, LINDA

Performer. Hopkins has had many successful performances in Paris since her show *Black and Blue* debuted in 1996. Her latest was *Wild Woman Blues* in 2001.

HORNE, LENA

Singer. Horne was one of many celebrity artists to perform at Chez Honey, the gallery-night spot owned by Herbert Gentry and his wife Honey Johnson. The club was open from 1947 to 1949.

HOWARD, NOAH

Musician. Howard was a member of the Frank Wright quartet. The group played in Paris during the 1970s.

HUGHES, LANGSTON

Poet, playwright and author. Works include *The Big Sea* (autobiography) and *Ways of White Folks* (short stories). Part of the Black Montmartre scene, Hughes arrived in Paris in 1924. He traveled in Europe, then to the US, and returned to France in 1937. His writings were considered important to those in Paris who had launched the *Négritude* movement.

HUNTER, ALBERTA

Singer. Hunter performed in Paris and in other Western European countries during the 1930s, as well as in the Middle East and Russia.

IVY, JAMES

Editor. Ivy was a participant in the Congress of Negro Artists and Writers held at the Sorbonne in 1956 and was elected vice president of the *Société Africaine de Culture* in the same year.

JACKMAN, HAROLD

Philanthropist. A very good friend of Countee Cullen, Jackman visited Paris for the first time in 1925. He returned for an extended visit during the summer of 1928.

JACKSON, JESSE

Minister, civil rights leader. The Reverend Jackson went to Paris in 1999 with the intent of building contacts with the private sector of the African-American community in Paris. Photographer Kim Powell-Jaulin chronicled his visit with her camera.

JACKSON, MAHALIA

Performer. Jackson had a very successful performance at the Olympia Music Hall in 1961.

JOANS, TED

Surrealist poet and artist. Works include *Teducation* and *All of Ted Joans and No More*. Joans first went to Paris in 1960 and was proclaimed the first African-American surrealist by his idol, André Breton. Having learned of the movement as a child, Joans traveled to Paris to become a part of it. He now travels frequently between the US, Africa, and France.

JOHNSON, JACK

Boxer. Johnson fought several boxing matches in Paris during the 1910s, and was well known and respected in Paris's Black Montmartre.

JOHNSON, NICOLE

Business manager. A manager of Fashion Fair Cosmetics during the 1990s, Johnson also was instrumental in the launching of Percy's Place, an African-American-owned restaurant and tea room in Paris.

JOHNSON, WILLIAM H.

Artist. Johnson studied in Paris from 1926 to 1927 using funds raised by his mentor, Charles Webster Hawthorne. He chose to work mostly on his own, studying works in museums such as the Louvre and the Jeu de Paume while making sketches and expanding his creative vision.

JONES, FLORENCE

Performer. The first female African-American entertainer in Paris, Jones and her husband Palmer were well known in Black Montmartre during the interwar years.

JONES, LOÏS MAILOU

Artist. Works include *Les Fetiches* and *Les Pommes Vertes*. The most prominent female African-American artist of her time, Jones was inspired by Meta Warwick Fuller to go to Paris to fulfill her artistic aspirations. She received a fellowship to study at the Académie Julian in 1937, and moved to the City of Light for the first of many extended visits there.

JONES, PALMER

Musician. Jones was the piano player at Louis Mitchell's club in Black Montmartre during the interwar years.

JONES, QUINCY

Musician, composer. Jones was a *protegé* of the famous Nadia Boulanger, with whom he studied composition and counterpoint in the 1950s. He received the French Legion of Honor award in 1990.

KAIRSON, URSULINE

Performer. Kairson has performed at the cabaret Paradis Latin for over sixteen years. She moved to Paris in 1983.

KILGORE, DAVIDA

Author. Kilgore spent her first years in Paris in 1989 and 1990 and returned in 1992 to participate in the "African Americans and Europe" conference held at the Sorbonne.

KING, MARTIN LUTHER, JR.

Minister, civil rights leader. King visited Paris in 1965 to speak at the American Cathedral and the Salle de la Mutualité.

LACY, MADISON D.

Producer/director. Works include the award-winning series *Eyes on the Prize II* and *Richard Wright – Black Boy.* Lacy visited Paris in 1991 and 1992.

LAPLANTE, PATRICIA

Promoter of African-American culture. Laplante is the creator of the African-American Literary Soirée, which features African-American writers of all genres of literature. She also hosts Paris Connections, a weekly Sunday dinner that often highlights African-American achievement of all types.

LAWRENCE, JACOB

Artist. Lawrence was honored at the 1994 conference "A Visual Arts Encounter: African Americans and Europe" by having his likeness placed on t-shirts that were distributed to all participants. Lawrence was unable to attend the conference due to illness.

LEWIS, REGINALD

Attorney, business mogul. Lewis bought TLC Beatrice, an enormous French food company, in 1987. He moved his family to Paris in 1988.

LION, JULES

Artist. Lion was a student at the Ecole des Beaux-Arts from approximately 1833 to 1836. Several of his lithographs were exhibited at Paris salons in 1831, 1834, and 1836. He moved to New Orleans in 1836 or 1837.

LOCKE, ALAIN

Educator, Rhodes Scholar, author of *The New Negro.* Locke visited Paris several times during the summers of the 1920s and 30s. The summer of 1924 was spent in the company of Langston Hughes, who he hoped would contribute a written work to the magazine that he was editing.

LOGAN, RAYFORD

Historian. Logan was appointed deputy secretary of the Pan-African Association created in 1921. He was a participant in the Pan-African Congress held that year in Paris.

LOVING, AL

Artist. Loving was a participant in the "Living American Artists" exhibit held in 1970 in Paris.

MAJOR, CLARENCE

Author, artist. Major visited Paris in 1982 and was inspired to write his poem "Home on Rue du Bourg-Tibourg."

MALCOLM X

Civil rights activist. Malcolm X visited France in 1964, when he stopped in Paris to address a crowd at the Salle de la Mutualité. He returned in February of the following year, but for political reasons he was not permitted to enter the country.

MARROW, ESTHER "QUEEN ESTHER"

Performer. Marrow and her Harlem Gospel Singers performed at the Théâtre Mogador in Paris in 1995.

MATHEUS, JOHN F.

Educator, author, contributor to the New Negro movement. Matheus studied at the Sorbonne in 1925.

MCKAY, CLAUDE

Poet, author. Works include *Banjo* and *A Long Way to Come Home* (autobiography). McKay arrived in Paris in 1923 and lived there during the mid-1920s. He spent a great deal of time in the provinces of France.

MCKENDRICK, MIKE

Musician. McKendrick was the banjo player in the group appearing with Sidney Bechet at Chez Florence; he and Bechet had a gun battle in 1928.

MERCER, MABEL

Performer. Mercer headlined for Bricktop in the club that Bricktop opened on rue Pigalle in 1931.

MIDDLETON, SAM

Artist. Middleton lived in Paris from 1961 to 1963, and was described by Ted Joans as "…the Afro-American *numero uno* modern artist in Europe."

MILLER, R. D.

Tailor. Miller was one of the black business owners in Black Montmartre during the interwar years.

MILLS, FLORENCE

Performer. Mills performed at Les Ambassadeurs in Paris in 1926, and returned to dazzle audiences in the 1927 musical revue *Blackbirds*.

MITCHELL, LOUIS

Band leader, restaurateur. Mitchell played a role in introducing jazz to Paris in 1917, and became very active in Black Montmartre during the 1920s as a night club and restaurant owner.

MONNERVILLE, GASTON

Former President of the French Sénat. French Guiana native Monnerville and his wife hosted pianist Philippa Schuyler on the Palais du Luxembourg in 1955 during his tenure as president of the Sénat.

MORRISON, TONI

Author, educator. Works include *Sula*, *The Bluest Eye*, *Beloved*, and *Paradise*. A frequent visitor to Paris, Morrison has held many readings and book signings of her work, and she taught a seminar at the College de France during the 1990s.

MOTLEY, ARCHIBALD

Artist. A scholarship from the Guggenheim Foundation allowed Motley and his wife to visit Paris for one year. His favorite subjects for painting were the characters that he found in nightclubs and dance halls. One of his paintings featured the Jockey Club (1929), where many Americans hung out.

NARDAL SISTERS (PAULETTE, JANE, AND ANDRÉE)

Participators in the foundation of the *Négritude* movement. These women from Martinique held a salon for black intellectuals in their 5th *arrondissement* home, and played an integral part in the *Négritude* movement in Paris.

NICHOLAS, ALBERT

Musician. A jazz clarinetist who performed in Paris during the 1950s, Nicholas was a friend of James Baldwin.

NICHOLAS BROTHERS

Dancers. These dance artists were featured at the Olympia Music Hall and the now defunct Club des Champs-Elysées.

NORMAN, JESSYE

Singer. Norman is a greatly appreciated opera singer in France. In 1984, she was awarded the *Commandeur des Arts et des Lettres*, and in 1989, President François Mitterand awarded her the French Legion of Honor.

PARKER, CHARLIE

Musician. Parker, sublime bebop jazzman, headlined with Sidney Bechet at the International Paris Jazz Festival in 1949.

PARKS, GORDON

Photographer, film director, author. Works include *Shaft* and *The Learning Tree* (autobiographical novel). Parks and Richard Wright lunched at Maxim's together in 1959.

PAYNE, DANIEL A.

Bishop of the AME church, educator. Payne attended the World Antislavery Conference in Paris in 1857 and returned twice more before the end of the year, in September and November. His November visit lasted until April 1858. He returned again in 1881.

PAYNTER, JOHN H.

Author, civil servant. Works include *The Fugitives of the Pearl, Fifty Years After*, and *Joining the Navy*. Paynter visited Paris in 1936, and wrote extensively of his stay in his book *Fifty Years After*.

PORTER, CHARLES ETHAN

Artist. Porter went to Paris in 1881 with a letter of introduction written by Mark Twain. He was a student at the Ecole des Beaux-Arts and exhibited his works at many Paris salons. He remained there until 1884, when he returned to the United States.

POTTER, LARRY

Artist. Potter first visited Paris in 1956, returned briefly to the US in 1958 and almost immediately returned to Paris. His art became increasingly abstract as he absorbed the influence of many Paris artists. He had a successful gallery exhibition in 1964, and continued to paint until his death from an asthma attack in 1966. He died in Paris.

POWELL, BUD

Musician. Powell went to Paris in 1959 and regaled the French with his talent at the keyboard. He worked in jazz clubs until he contracted tuberculosis in 1962.

POWELL-JAULIN, KIM

Photographer. Connecticut-born Powell-Jaulin has degrees in chemistry and construction management. She has pursued her passion for photography since she moved to Paris with her French husband and daughter in 1992.

PRICE, LEONTYNE

Singer. Price has headlined at the Palais Garnier, the oldest remaining French opera house, several times. She starred in *Aida* there in 1968.

PRICE-MARS, JEAN

President of the *Société Africaine de Culture*. A native of Haiti, Price-Mars was elected the first president of the African Culture Society in 1956.

PROPHET, NANCY ELIZABETH

Artist. Works include *Negro Head* and *Congolais*. Prophet was supported by funding from the Carnegie Foundation, enrolled at the Ecole des Beaux-Arts in Paris, and had success in both exhibiting and selling her work there. She lived in Paris from 1922 to 1934.

REED, ISHMAEL

Author. Prolific writer Reed was one of the participants at the 1992 Sorbonne conference "African Americans and Europe."

RINGGOLD, FAITH

Artist. Ringgold was one of the participants in the 1994 conference "A Visual Arts Encounter: African Americans and Europe," at which she shared recollections of her first visit to Paris in 1961 with the participants. She eventually created a quilt based on a fantasy born of that visit.

RIVERS, HAYWARD "BILL"

Artist. One of the many African-American artists to come to Paris on the GI Bill, Rivers arrived in 1949. He, along with several other artists, eventually founded a co-op called the Galerie Huit, where black artists could exhibit their work.

ROBESON, PAUL

Performer, political activist. A visitor to Paris from the 1920s to the 1950s, Robeson was a celebrated guest among members, including Gertrude Stein and Sylvia Beach, of the "American colony." He performed in concert and spoke at politically-oriented conferences.

ROGERS, JOEL AUGUSTUS

Journalist. Rogers was a correspondent for the African-American press who went to Paris in the 1920s to chronicle the lives of American blacks there.

SAUNDERS, RAYMOND

Artist, educator. Saunders' paintings were exhibited at the Musée des Arts Décoratifs in the 1980s. He had two solo exhibits at the Galerie Resche in 1990 and 1991. As a professor at the California College of Arts and Crafts, Saunders continues to bring American art students to Paris each summer.

SAVAGE, AUGUSTA

Artist. Savage had a very productive period during her Paris years. In 1930, a French publication featured four of her sculptures and she exhibited at the Salon d'Automne. She exhibited at this salon again in 1931, as well as at the Colonial Exposition of 1931 where she received a gold medallion for her sculpture entitled *Amazon*.

SCHUYLER, PHILIPPA

Pianist and composer. A child prodigy born of an African-American father and an Anglo-American mother, Schuyler debuted in Paris in 1955. She performed in over eighty countries throughout the world.

SCOTT, WILLIAM EDOUARD

Artist. Scott went to Paris in 1909, studied at the Julian Academy for a year, and was mentored by Henry O. Tanner in Etaples. As a result, he showed his works successfully at a salon in Toquet in 1911. He was bestowed a great honor the following year when his painting *The Poor Neighbor* was critically acclaimed in France and purchased by the government of Argentina.

SÉJOUR, VICTOR

Playwright. Louisiana-born Séjour enjoyed success as a playwright in Paris during the 1850s and 60s.

SENGHOR, LÉOPOLD SEDAR

Former president of Senegal. As a young writer in Paris, Senghor participated in the gatherings hosted by the Nardal Sisters where African, Caribbean, and American blacks met and discussed various aspects of black culture. These meetings took place during the years 1929-1934, and were part of the launching of the *Négritude* movement.

SIMONE, NINA

Performer. A singer, pianist, arranger and composer, Simone has known great success in France. Aside from living in Paris for a time and giving several performances over the years, she recorded her album *Fodder on My Wings* in the City of Light in 1982.

SIMPSON, COREEN

Photographer, jewelry designer. Creator of *The Black Cameo*. Simpson worked as a fashion photographer in Paris during the 1960s.

SIMPSON, LORNA

Photographer. Critically acclaimed Simpson was one of the artists who was invited to participate in the February 1994 conference "A Visual Arts Encounter."

SIMPSON, MERTON

Artist, musician. Simpson has exhibited his art and played jazz saxaphone in the French capital. His group played at the memorial of Larry Potter in 1966, and his paintings were exhibited at a 6th *arrondissement* gallery in 1992.

SISSLE, NOBLE

Musician, orchestra leader. Sissle was the drum major for James Europe's 369th Infantry band. It was this group that brought jazz to France during World War I. Sissle returned to Paris to give several concerts in the late 1920s.

SMITH, ADA "BRICKTOP"

Performer, nightclub owner. The queen of Black Paris in the years between World Wars I and II, Bricktop made a name for herself first as a performer and then as a nightclub owner. She entertained royalty and commoners alike in her clubs.

SMITH, ALBERT ALEXANDER

Artist, musician. Smith performed as a jazz musician in various places around Paris during the 1930s to support himself while pursuing his art. He also sold prints of various city street scenes and monuments.

SMITH, WILLIAM GARDNER

Author, journalist. Works include *Return to Black America* and *The Stone Face*. Smith spent most of the 1950s and 60s in Paris, marrying twice and writing two novels. One of these was *The Stone Face*, in which Smith portrays black expatriate life in 1950s Paris.

STEVENSON, IRIS

Choir leader. Stevenson and her choir have contributed greatly to the popularity that gospel music enjoys in Paris today. She brought her group to Europe at least twice during the 1990s and played to exalted crowds in the American Cathedral of Paris.

TANNER, HENRY O.

Artist. Works include *The Thankful Poor* and *The Banjo Lesson*. The pioneer African-American artist, Tanner went to Paris in 1891 after having studied at the Pennsylvania Academy of Fine Arts. He became a role model for dozens of black American painters who followed his example and went to Paris to pursue their art.

TERRELL, MARY CHURCH

Civil and women's rights activist. Terrell visited Paris in 1888, 1904, and 1919. She undertook her visit in 1919 as a delegate to the International Peace Congress.

VAN BRACKEN, FRANK

Journalist. Van Bracken was the Paris correspondent for *Ebony* magazine during the 1950s.

VAN PEEBLES, MELVIN

Author, filmmaker. Films include *Watermelon Man* and *Sweet Sweetback's Baadasssss Song*. Van Peebles worked in Paris as a literary critic and as a cartoonist before successfully publishing several books in the mid-1960s. He directed his first film in Paris in 1967, and was awarded the Legion of Honor in 2001.

WALKER, T-BONE

Musician. A blues guitarist, Walker was part of the Paris jazz craze of the post-World War II era. He performed in several places during the late 1960s.

WARING, LAURA WHEELER

Artist. This artist studied in Paris from 1924 to 1925 on a scholorship from the Pennsylvania Academy of Fine Arts.

WELDON, MAXINE

Performer. Weldon enjoyed successful runs in live Paris musicals during the 1990s and in 2001.

WELLS, MONIQUE Y.

Veterinary pathologist, entrepreneur, author. Works include *Food for the Soul* and ***Paris Reflections.*** Wells and her husband came to Paris in 1992. They created the travel service called Discover Paris! – Personalized Itineraries for Independent Travelers. Wells' books are the fruits of her experiences in Paris.

WEST, CORNEL

Educator. Harvard professor West visited Paris in 2000 to address a gathering of African Americans in the place of Henry Louis Gates, who was too ill to travel for the occasion.

WIDEMAN, JOHN EDGAR

Novelist. Rhodes scholar. Works include *Brothers and Keepers*, *A Glance Away*, and *The Cattle Killing*. Wideman's works have been published by the French publishing house Gallimard. He visits Paris from time to time to read from his works and to visit friends.

WILLIAMS, JOHN A.

Author, journalist. Williams was the European correspondent for *Ebony* and *Jet* in the 1960s. He returned to Paris in 1992 for the Sorbonne conference "African Americans and Europe."

WILLIAMS, MICHAEL KELLY

Artist. Williams had his work exhibited in Paris in 1951, 1953, and 1955.

WILLIAMS, SHIRLEY ANNE

Author and literary critic. Works include *Girls Together*, *Working Cotton*, and *Deesa Rose*. Williams was another of the participants in the "African Americans and Europe" conference in 1992.

WILSON, JOHN

Artist. Wilson came to Paris during the 1950s to study with Fernand Léger.

WOODRUFF, HALE

Artist. Woodruff was the recipient of the first Harmon Foundation award in 1926, and used this money to travel to France to study.

WOODSON, CARTER G.

Historian, educator, author. One of many African Americans to study at the Sorbonne, Woodson attended courses for a semester in 1907.

WRIGHT, ALBERTA

Restaurateur. Soul food was served once again on the Left Bank when Wright opened Jezebel's in 1990. The restaurant closed four years later.

WRIGHT, BRUCE MCMARION

Poet, attorney. Works include *Repetitions* and *Beyond the Blues*. Wright created several poems in Paris from 1958 up to the 1990s.

WRIGHT, FRANK

Musician. In 1967, in Paris, Wright, Muhammad Ali, and Bobby Few created the record label called "Center of the World."

WRIGHT, JULIA

Political activist, daughter of Richard Wright. Wright moved to Paris with her parents in 1946. She is an advocate for the abolition of the death penalty and a champion of her father's works.

WRIGHT, RICHARD

Author. Works include *Native Son* and *Black Boy*. Aside from James Baldwin, Wright is the best known African-American author to settle in Paris during the post-World-War-II years. He lived in Paris from 1947 until his death in 1960.

YOUNG, ANDREW

Former mayor of Atlanta, Georgia. The mayor had the honor of inaugurating the "Atlanta in France" exhibition at the Sorbonne in 1985.

YOUNG, LESTER

Musician. Saxaphonist Young was one of many jazz musicians who played in Paris during the 1950s.

For Additional Information

BOOKS, MAGAZINES, AND CATALOGS

Archer-Straw, P. 2000. *Negrophilia*. London: Thames & Hudson.

Anonymous. 1966. "A Transoceanic 'Happy Birthday'." *Ebony* 21 (4): 54-60.

Bernard, C. 1989. *Afro American Artists in Paris: 1919-1939*. New York: Hunter College Galleries.

Bomani, A., and B. Rooks, editors. 1992. *Paris Connections: African-American Artists in Paris*. San Francisco: Q.E.D. Press.

Buffalo, A., editor. 1996. *Explorations in the City of Light: African-American Artists in Paris, 1945-1965*. New York: Studio Museum of Harlem.

Daix, P. 1977. *La Vie de Peintre de Pablo Picasso*. Paris: Editions du Seuil.

Fabre, M. 1991. *From Harlem to Paris – Black American Writers in France, 1840-1980*. Urbana and Chicago: University of Illinois Press.

Fabre, M., and J. A. Williams. 1996. *A Street Guide to African Americans in Paris*. Paris and Belleville Lake Press: Cercle d'Etudes Afro-Americaines.

Glyn, A. 2000. *The Companion Guide to Paris*. Woodbridge: Companion Guides.

Himes, C. 1976. *My Life of Absurdity*. New York: Thunder's Mouth Press.

Klüver, B., and J. Martin. 1989. *Kiki et Montparnasse, 1900-1930*. New York: Harry N. Abrams, Incorporated.

Lewis, R. F., and B. S. Walker. 1994. *Why Should White Guys Have All the Fun?* New York: John Wiley & Sons.

Lloyd, C. 2000. *Eugene Bullard – Black Expatriate in Jazz Age Paris*. Athens: University of Georgia Press.

Low, W .A., and V. A. Clift, editors. 1981. *Encyclopedia of Black America*. New York: Da Capo Press.

Mack, T. 2000. "Racisme déjà vu." *Emerge* 11 (8): 48-52.

Stovall, T. 1996. *Paris Noir – African Americans in the City of Light*. New York: Mariner Books.

Vallois, T. 1995. *Around and About Paris, Volume 1*. London: Iliad Books.

_____. 1996. *Around and About Paris, Volume 2*. London: Iliad Books.

_____. 1997. *Around and About Paris – New Horizons: Haussmann's Annexation*. London: Iliad Books.

White, N. 1991. *The Guide to the Architecture of Paris*. New York: Charles Schribner's Sons.

WEB REFERENCES

Arneaux, J. A. – virtual.clemson.edu/caah/shakespr/projects/bbyrd/shake4.htm; docsouth.unc.edu/neh/simmons/simmons.html

Baldwin, James (Legion of Honor) – www.gaygate.com/media/pages/JamesBa.shtml

Billops and Hatch – www.varoregistry.com/billops/bio.html

Braxton, Anthony – www.lovely.com/bios/braxton.html

Cardin, Pierre – www.celebritytrendz.com/fashion/designers/pierrecardin1.html

Césaire, Aimé – monthlyreview.org/1199kell.htm; www.africana.com/tt_242.htm; www.iupjournals.org/ral/ral29-3.html

Delaney, Beauford (and Henry Miller) – www.sunsite.utk.edu/delaney/neely.htm

Fernandez, Armand Pierre – www.arman-studio.com/

Grosvenor, Vertamae – www.npr.org/programs/seasonings/Vertamae.html

Harmon, David – www.pcfandp.com/a/p/8401/s.html

Happersberger, Lucien – www.gaygate.com/media/pages/JamesBa.shtml

Hunter, Alberta – www.blueflamecafe.com/default.htm

Jones, Loïs Mailou – www.people.virginia.edu/~emw9f/callaloo/mailoujones.html

Jones, Quincy – http://www.duke.edu/~jcf3/

La Reine Blanche – www.nytimes.com/books/first/o/olney-reflexions.html

Ringgold, Faith – www.madisonartcenter.org/ringgold/ringgold.htm

Schuyler, Philippa – www.africana.com/tt_056.htm

Senghor, Léopold – www.outremer44.org/article1.htm

Simone, Nina – ninasimone.com/nina.html

Williams, Shirley Anne – www.cc.emory.edu/ENGLISH/Bahri/ AfricanAmerican.html

Wright, Frank – www.centrohd.com/music/allmusic/art1.htm

Travel Tips

AIRPORTS

There are two main airports in Paris: Roissy-Charles de Gaulle (16 miles or 25.75 kilometers to the north) and Orly (about the same distance to the south). Both airports can be reached from the center of the city by bus or taxi in about 45 minutes, depending on traffic conditions. Limousine service, commercial shuttles, and public transportation are also available for access to Paris. Regional trains provide the most rapid service, except during peak commute hours (7:00 to 9:00 AM and 5:00 to 7:00 PM on weekdays) when there may be significant delays. It is always best to play it safe and allow at least an hour to reach your destination.

ROISSY-CHARLES DE GAULLE AIRPORT

Roissy is the larger of the two main airports in Paris. It has two principal terminals, Charles de Gaulle 1 and Charles de Gaulle 2.

AIRLINES

Air France	US: 1-800-237-2747	Paris: 0.820.820.820
American	US: 1-800-433-7300	Paris: 0.801.872.872
Continental	US: 1-800-525-0280	Paris: 01.42.99.09.09
Delta	US: 1-800-221-1212	Paris: 0.800.35.40.80
Lufthansa	US: 1-800-645-3880	Paris: 0.802.020.030
Northwest	US: 1-800-225-2525	Paris: 0.810.55.65.56
TWA	US: 1-800-433-7300	Paris: 0.801.892.892
United	US: 1-800-241-6522	Paris: 0.801.62.62.62
US Airways	US: 1-800-428-4322	Paris: 0.801.63.22.22

GENERAL INFORMATION

Airport Information	Paris: 0.836.68.15.15
Airport Security	Paris: 01.48.62.31.22

Customs and Immigration	Paris: 01.48.62.62.85
Lost and Found	Paris: 01.48.62.13.34 (CDG1)
	01.48.16.63.83 (CDG2)

RENTAL CARS

Avis	Paris: 01.48.62.34.34 (CDG1)	01.48.62.59.59 (CDG2)
Budget	Paris: 01.48.62.70.21 (CDG1)	01.48.62.70.22 (CDG2)
Europcar	Paris: 01.48.62.33.33 (CDG1)	01.48.62.56.47 (CDG2)
Hertz	Paris: 01.48.62.29.00 (CDG1)	01.48.62.69.22 (CDG2)
National Citer	Paris: 01.48.62.65.81 (CDG1)	01.48.62.64.84 (CDG2)
Sixt Eurorent	Paris: 01.48.62.40.77 (CDG1)	01.48.62.57.66 (CDG2)

ORLY AIRPORT

Orly Airport has two terminals, Orly Sud (South) and Orly Ouest (West).

AIRLINES

| Air France | US: 1-800-237-2747 | Paris: 0.820.820.820 |
| Lufthansa | US: 1-800-645-3880 | Paris: 0.802.020.030 |

GENERAL INFORMATION

Airport Information	Paris: 01.49.75.15.15
Airport Security	Paris: 01.49.75.43.04
Customs	Paris: 01.49.75.09.10
Lost and Found	Paris: 01.49.75.34.10 (South)
	01.49.75.42.34 (West)

RENTAL CARS

Avis	Paris: 01.49.75.44.91 (South) / 01.49.75.56.20 (West)
Budget	Paris: 01.49.75.56.61 (South) / 01.49.75.56.04 (West)
Europcar	Paris: 01.49.75.47.42 (South) / 01.49.75.47.46 (West)
Hertz	Paris: 01.49.75.84.48 (South) / 01.49.75.84.57 (West)
National/Citer	Paris: 01.49.75.36.57 (South) / 01.49.75.36.36 (West)
Sixt Eurorent	Paris: 01.49.75.50.01 (South) / 01.49.75.50.83 (West)

A WORD ABOUT RENTING CARS

If you have a love for death-defying adventure, rent a car and drive around the Arc de Triomphe, Bastille, or any number of other busy Parisian roundabouts. Even the most well-dressed, sophisticated Parisian becomes your worst nightmare behind the wheel of a car. *Any car entering from the right has the right-of-way.* Fasten your seat belts because you can be fined upwards of 152 Euros, or roughly $140.00, if you don't.

ARRONDISSEMENTS: LEFT BANK / RIGHT BANK

The twenty *arrondissements* or districts of Paris unwind from a clockwise spiral, with the oldest and smallest found in the center. The 1st through 4th and the 8th *arrondissements* are found on the Right Bank and the 5th through 7th *arrondissements* are on the Left Bank.

Because it has fewer monuments and more narrow, twisting streets, many areas of the Left Bank have more charm than the Right Bank. The Left Bank is still considered a symbol of Bohemian life, a meeting place for thinkers, artists, writers, and others. It is on the Left Bank where you will find the most unique outdoor cafés and bookstores. The 7th *arrondissement* is an exception to this general rule; here you will find many foreign embassies and consulates as well as the colossal Hôtel des Invalides that houses Napoleon Bonaparte's tomb.

In contrast, the Right Bank has more architecture representative of royal power and authority. The magnificent Louvre and the grandiose Palais Garnier are just a couple of examples. When the wealthy bourgeoisie built their homes in the outlying areas of the Right Bank they naturally wanted the facades, courtyards, and interiors of their dwellings to be comparable to those of royal stature. Thus it is common to find vast stretches of ornate, carved buildings and perfect squares such as place des Vosges, place François I, and place Vendôme to the north of the Seine.

The 9th through 11th *arrondissements* lie neither in the innermost nor the outermost part of the spiral. They are found immediately to the north and east of the 2nd, 3rd, and 4th *arrondissements*. Some beautiful *hôtels particuliers,* or mansions, may be found in the 9th *arrondissement*, as it was initially developed by and for wealthy people. On the outer edge of the spiral are the highest numbers, beginning with the twelfth and ending with the twentieth. The 13th *arrondissement* is considered Paris's Chinatown; it features many Asian shops and restaurants. The inhabitants of the 12th and the 14th through 17th districts are largely French, from the working class to the wealthy. And from the 18th to the 20th *arrondissements*, the City of Light becomes Ethnic Paris, a rich mosaic of many of the world's cultures. There you will find charming Parisian villages with cobblestone streets and quiet squares, as well as authentic North African, Asian, and West African restaurants hidden amongst the scattering of modern high rises.

BUSINESS HOURS

Business hours are generally Monday through Friday from 9:00 AM to 5:00 PM and Saturday from 10:00 AM to 7:00 PM. Smaller shops and banks close for one to two hours for lunch. Some places may open on Sunday for half a day, and if a shop is open Sunday it will likely be closed Monday. Some banks may also open on Saturday mornings.

August in Paris is still known for the *fermeture annuelle*, the time when many Parisians enthusiastically leave Paris for the country or the seashore. They leave many shops and restaurants closed in their wake, but as time passes more and more restaurants and shops remain open during this period.

CHANGING MONEY

Money can be exchanged at airports, train stations, change offices *(Bureaux de Change),* and banks throughout the city. Banks that exchange foreign currency will display a sign reading CHANGE in the window or on the door. *Bureau de Change* offices vary in the services and rates that they offer. Some charge a service fee. All change offices will display a sign that reads either *Commission Chargé* or *No Commission.* Travelers' checks can be exchanged as long as you present your passport as identification. You can also obtain local currency by using an ATM machine *(distributeur automatique),* but before placing your credit card in one of these, look for the decals on the machine that indicate what types of cards it accepts.

If you find yourself with lots of cash and the banks are closed, you can also change money at the train stations **Gare d'Austerlitz** (until 5:00 PM), **Gare de l'Est** (until 7:00 PM), **Gare Saint Lazare** (until 8:00 PM), and **Gare de Lyon** (until 11:00 PM). See **RAILWAY STATIONS** for locations.

Note: Exchange rates listed in newspapers are not necessarily those found on the exchange board at the *Bureau de Change.*

CONSULATE

If you find yourself in the unfortunate position of having your passport lost or stolen, replacement forms and information can be found at the American Consulate:

2, rue Saint-Florentin
75001 Paris
Tel: 01.43.12.48.40

Presenting a photocopy of the first page of your passport will expedite replacement procedures. Consular services are available from 9:00 AM to 3:00 PM on weekdays.

The American Embassy is located at:
2, rue avenue Gabriel
75008 Paris
Tel: 01.43.12.22.22

Both the Consulate and the Embassy are closed on American holidays.

CURRENCY

The Euro (€), Europe's new currency, replaced the French franc in February 2002. Bills currently in circulation are 500 €, 200 €, 100 €, 50 €, 20 €, 10€ and 5€. Coins currently in circulation are: 2 €, 1 €, 50 euro centimes, 20 euro centimes, 10 euro centimes, 5 euro centimes, 2 euro centimes and 1 euro centime.

Both the bills and the coins differ in size and/or color by denomination. The front of each coin has the same design for all 12 countries in the euro area. The reverse side displays different designs for each country, created by their own national artists. All exchange rates for the Euro are listed at *Bureau de Change* offices.

DATE AND TIME

In France, the date is written by placing the day first, then the month, followed by the year. So May 10, 2001 is written 10/5/01 instead of 5/10/01 as would be done in the US. France also uses the 24-hour clock, so 2:00 PM becomes 14h00 (the 'h' means *heure* or hour). Time differences between Paris and the US range from 6 to 9 hours depending on the time zone in the US.

DRESS

The French have a reputation for always being smartly dressed in public. They have a way of carrying themselves that can make the average Frenchman look as though he is wearing the finest Armani. But the truth is that the caliber of dress depends a great deal on where in Paris you are, and what you define as smart dress.

There is far more flexibility in what is accepted public attire than is widely believed. But having said this, we recommend that you leave the jogging suits at home. Many people in Paris opt for lightweight linens or similar fabrics as an alternative to shorts.

In the following tables of equivalent sizes, French sizes have been rounded up where necessary. It is always better to have clothes a little too big than too tight.

FRENCH AND US CLOTHING SIZES

WOMEN'S DRESSES, KNITWEAR, AND BLOUSES

F	36	38	40	42	44	46	48
US	8	10	12	14	16	18	20

WOMEN'S STOCKINGS

F	1	2	3	4	5
US	8	9	10	11	12

WOMEN'S SHOES

F	35	36	37	38	39	40	41
US	6	6½	7	7½	8	9	10

MEN'S SHOES

F	39	40	41	42	43	44	45
US	6	7	7½	8½	9	10	11

MEN'S SUITS

F	36	38	40	42	44	46	48
US	35	36	37	38	39	40	42

MEN'S SHIRTS

F	36	37	38	39	40	41	42
US	14	14½	15	15½	16	16½	17

MEN'S SWEATERS

F	36	38	40	42	44	46
US	46	48	51	54	56	59

Note: For shoe and sock sizes the French use the word *pointure*, so a size 37 shoe is *une chaussure pointure 37*. For all other types of garments (even stockings and tights) the word *taille* is used, so a size 16 shirt is *une chemise taille 40,* etc.

ELECTRICITY

Electricity in France is 220 volts and 50 cycles versus that in the US which is 110 volts and 60 cycles. If you plan to stay in a charming little hotel as far away from the average tourist as possible, be sure to bring an electricity converter for your hair dryer or electric shaver. If you are planning to bring your electric curling iron or hot-comb, be sure that your converter is specifically designed for items that "heat up." If you are uncertain about your converter, test your hot-comb or curler on a piece of fabric or towel *before* putting it on your hair.

ENGLISH LANGUAGE MEDIA

Most major hotels offer cable television which includes CNN and the CBS Nightly News.

You can also listen to English language radio on the following stations:

BBC Radio Four (1,500 LW)
BBC World Service (29.0 MHz)

ENGLISH LANGUAGE PUBLICATIONS / BOOKSTORES

The *International Herald Tribune, The Wall Street Journal, USA Today,* and several British newspapers are widely available in central Paris and at certain English language bookstores, some of which are:

W. H. Smith
248, rue de Rivoli
75001 Paris
Tel: 01.44.77.88.99

Galignani
224, rue de Rivoli
75001 Paris
Tel: 01.42.60.76.07

Brentano's
37, avenue de l'Opéra
75002 Paris
Tel: 01.42.61.52.50

Other stores include Tea & Tattered Pages, The Village Voice, The San Francisco Book Company, Shakespeare & Company, and The Abbey Bookshop.

ENGLISH–SPEAKING PHARMACIES

Are you all out of your favorite mouthwash? Have you had a few too many delightful French treats during the day? Maybe all you need is an aspirin. Fortunately, there are several English language pharmacies in Paris, including:

Pharmacie Les Champs
(open 24 hours a day, 7 days a week)
84, avenue des Champs-Elysées
75008 Paris
Tel: 01.45.62.02.41

Pharmacie Anglaise
62, avenue des Champs-Elysées
75008 Paris
Tel: 01.43.59.22.52

Pharmacie Swann
6, rue Castiglione
75001 Paris
Tel: 01.42.60.72.96

British & American Pharmacy
1, rue Auber
75009 Paris
Tel: 01.42.65.88.29

HEALTH / MEDICAL ASSISTANCE

Paris also has services available for problems of a more serious nature.

American Hospital (English-speaking)
63, boulevard Victor Hugo
92202 Neuilly-sur-Seine
Tel: 01.47.47.70.15

Franco-British Hospital (English-speaking)
3, rue Barbès
92300 Levallois-Perret
Tel: 01.46.39.22.22

SOS HELP – psychological support and advice in English. Tel: 01.47.23.80.80 from 3:00 PM to 11:00 PM.

MARKETS

Paris has some of the most beautiful open-air markets in Europe. The vendors take pride in their stalls and try to make them more attractive than those of their rivals. There are over 100 street markets offering a variety of fresh foods. Here are just a few:

Place d'Auteuil, 16th *arrondissement*
Rue de Buci, 6th *arrondissement*
Rue Mouffetard, 5th *arrondissement*
Rue Poncelet, 17th *arrondissement*

Covered markets also sell fresh produce, meats, fish, and other items. Some examples are:

Aligre, place d'Aligre, 12th *arrondissement*: Tuesday-Saturday, Sunday morning.

Batignolles, 96, rue Lemercier, 17th *arrondissement*: Tuesday-Saturday, Sunday morning.

Enfants Rouges, 39, rue de Bretagne, 3rd *arrondissement*: Monday-Saturday, Sunday morning.

Saint Quentin, 85 bis, boulevard Magenta, 10th *arrondissement*: Tuesday-Saturday, Sunday morning.

Secrétan, 33, avenue Secrétan, 19th *arrondissement*: Monday-Saturday, Sunday morning.

For the avid flea-market addict, Paris can be a treasure chest of odd items. Silver lamps and picture frames from Poland, lovely items from Morocco or West Africa, or French office supplies from the 1950s await you. You can often find your heart's desire being sold on a little square of carpet by the side of the road.

Porte de Montreuil (access via metro Porte de Montreuil): Saturday, Sunday, and Monday.

Porte de Vanves (avenue Georges Lafenestre; access via metro Porte de Vanves): second-hand clothes, pictures, some antiques: Saturday and Sunday.

Saint-Ouen (access via metro Porte-de-Clignancourt): the largest and best-known flea market in Paris comprises sixteen distinct markets: Saturday, Sunday, and Monday.

PARKS

After a day of shopping, eating, shopping, visiting museums, and shopping, you may want to take a stroll or just sit for a bit in a lovely park. Here is a selection of some of the most beautiful parks in Paris:

Parc des Buttes Chaumont, 19th *arrondissement*
Parc Monceau, 8th *arrondissement*
Parc Montsouris, 14th *arrondissement*
Jardin du Luxembourg, 6th *arrondissement*

PASSPORT / VISA

Only a passport is required for US citizens visiting France for less than three months.

POSTAL SERVICES

The French post office, *La Poste*, is open Mondays through Fridays from 8:00 AM to 7:00 PM and on Saturdays from 8:00 AM to 12 noon. The central post office is located at 52, rue du Louvre, 75001 Paris, and is open 24 hours a day. First class postage for a postcard or average sized letter to the US is 67 euro centimes (0.67 €).

Note: If you want to buy stamps, be sure to stand in the correct line so as not to waste your time queuing up at the window where Parisians pay their gas and telephone bills. Many French people also bank at the post office, so **patience is required**. If you are in a real hurry and only need stamps, you may also buy them at *tabacs* (tobacco shops) and at some hotels and newsstands.

PUBLIC TRANSPORTATION

Metro (Le Métropolitain)

Riding the metro is the quickest and easiest way to get around the city. It is considerably safer than much of the underground transportation in the US. There are fourteen metro lines that cross Paris and interconnect at various stations. Tickets may be purchased at the window located next to the turnstiles. If you plan to rely on public transportation to get around town for the majority of your stay, it will be more economical to purchase a *carnet* of ten tickets rather than individual tickets. To enter the system, you must insert a ticket into the turnstile, then retrieve it as you pass through. One ticket will serve for multiple connections as long as you remain in the system. You must keep your ticket with you during the entire length of your voyage, as metro agents may ask to see it at any time. If you cannot produce the ticket, you will be immediately fined.

Note: Pickpockets flock to tourists like fruit flies to ripe melons, and busy metro lines such as the number 1 line (La Defense to Château de Vincennes) are filled with them. Keep your eyes open and your hands on your valuables.

RER

The RER *(Réseau Express Régional)* is a kind of super-metro service run by the same body that governs the metro system. RER trains are larger than metro trains and travel farther outside the city limits. They operate under the same principle as the metro; in fact, each RER line connects directly with the metro system at one or more points along its route. All RER stations are shown on metro maps.

Be aware that because the RER travels farther than does the metro, a ticket for a distant destination will cost more than a ticket for a destination within the metro system. You must insert your ticket into a turnstile to leave as well as to enter the RER station, and if you have not paid enough money for your particular destination you will not be allowed to pass. Trains will not necessarily stop at each station, so you should be sure that a light indicates your destination on the list of stations that is suspended above the platform.

Bus

Though the metro is likely to get you to your destination more quickly, buses offer the benefit of allowing you to experience the beauty of Paris as you are transported from place to place. Thus, they are a far more pleasant mode of transportation if you are not pressed for time. You may use the same tickets for the bus that you use for the metro, and one ticket will take you anywhere in town. You can buy tickets from the driver upon boarding. Again, you must keep your ticket with you for the entire length of your journey.

Taking the bus can be a bit tricky, as multiple bus lines may stop at a given bus stop and you must take care to board the correct one. You must signal for the driver to stop as he/she will not know for which bus you are waiting. Maps of the bus lines are posted at each stop, so you have the opportunity to study the route of each bus serving that stop.

Railway Stations

Paris has six train stations that link it to the rest of France, continental Europe, and London (via the Channel Tunnel):

Paris Austerlitz: 7, boulevard de l'Hôpital, 13th *arrondissement*
Paris Est: place du 11novembre 1918, 10th *arrondissement*
Paris Lyon: rue de Lyon, place Louis-Armand, 12th *arrondissement*
Paris Montparnasse: 17, boulevard de Vaugirard, 15th *arrondissement*
Paris Nord: 19, rue Dunkerque, 10th *arrondissement*
Paris Saint-Lazare: 88, rue Saint-Lazare, 9th *arrondissement*

SALES TAX

The sales tax on most goods and services is 20.6% and a refund on a percentage of the sales tax is available upon leaving the European Union. This benefit is available only with a purchase of merchandise at participating stores that totals or exceeds ~183 €. The vendor should supply the appropriate forms for *détaxe*. Be aware that certain restrictions apply.

Before checking your luggage at the airline ticket counter you must present these forms to customs. The customs official in the last European Union country you visit before your return to the US may ask to see the merchandise for which you are claiming a tax refund.

TAXIS

Paris has roughly 15,000 taxis. They can usually be found at taxi stands with the exception of weekend nights, peak commute hours, and during transportation strikes. Hailing a cab can be difficult if you are not aware of a couple of rules.

Rule # 1. A taxi will not stop in the middle of the street to accept a passenger and will quite often pass you by if it is not driving curbside. Customers are plentiful in Paris and taxi drivers rarely make much of an effort to accommodate. It is best to locate a cab at a *borne d'appel* or taxi stand, usually found on the corner along larger thoroughfares. They are often identified by a street sign that says "taxi" or a kiosk-like post labeled *tête de station*. Note that taxis queue at these stands and it is not acceptable to pass up the first taxi in favor of the more pleasant looking cabby near the rear. The first taxi in line is **your** taxi.

Rule # 2. Jumping up and down in the middle of the street and waving your arms about in a wild manner is a surefire way to get a cabby to pass you by at top speed. Simply extend your arm when a cab is approaching. When the roof light is bright the taxi is available; a dim light means the cab is occupied. Don't be discouraged by these simple rules and keep in mind that the taxi drivers' behavior does not mean that they dislike tourists.

Taxi rates vary. Rates increase at night between the hours of 10:00 PM and 6:30 AM as well as on Sundays. This is also true if the taxi collects you at a train station, hotel, or outside the city. Rate information is posted in the window of the back seat of the cab. If you (or the hotel *concierge*) phone ahead for a cab, the meter starts running the moment the driver receives the call. The dispatcher will tell you how long it will take your taxi to arrive.

Helpful tip: After you have successfully hailed a cab, give the driver the address of your destination and mention the name of the nearest main street or metro station as well. This will reduce your chances of being taken for an unscheduled tour of Paris.

TELEPHONE

Making a phone call in Europe can be a nightmare if you are unfamiliar with the country codes, the seemingly endless numbers, and telephone card system. However, once you are armed with all the information you need, making a phone call can be easy.

When dialing France from the US you must first dial 011 to obtain an overseas line. You must then dial the French country code (33) followed by the regional code (1 for Paris), then the local eight-digit number. If you are in Paris and you wish to dial a local number, you must dial 01 followed by the local eight-digit number.

To phone the UK from France, dial the prefix 00-44 followed by the number (omitting the first zero in the local number). To dial the US from France, dial the prefix 00-1 followed by the area code and your party's local 7-digit number.

There are public telephones in various places along the streets. Most public phones require a phone card called a *télécarte*. These are available for purchase at metro stations, post office branches, and tobacconists (who also sell stamps). Tobacconists are recognizable by their diamond-shaped red *TABAC* signs. A few café and restaurant phones still accept coins with a minimum charge of 0.30 €.

TIPPING

How much to tip the waiter is a question about which you need not worry. A 15% service charge is generally included in restaurant bills. A little extra gratuity is warranted only if service is especially good. In the hotel, a bellhop will expect 1 Euro per bag, and the taxi driver should be tipped about 5-10% of the fare.

Note: If you take a taxi and have quite a bit of luggage, the driver may add an additional 1.50 Euros to the fare in addition to the money normally charged per bag.

TOURIST OFFICES

Maps of Paris, information about museums, metro maps, and more can be found at the Office du Tourisme de Paris located at:

127, avenue des Champs-Elysées
75008 Paris
Tel: 01.49.52.53.00

There are also tourist offices at railway stations in the city.

WEATHER

The climate in Paris is relatively cool with the average temperature in summer not quite reaching 80° F (26.6° C). Clouds and rain are frequent and it is best to keep an umbrella on hand. A few of the larger metro stations have small shops that conveniently sell purse-sized umbrellas. Temperatures are expressed in degrees Celsius in France and throughout Europe.

The following chart shows average temperatures in degrees Fahrenheit (Celsius):

January	34-43° (1-6°)	**July**	58-76° (15-25°)
February	34-45° (1-7°)	**August**	58-75° (14-24°)
March	39-54° (4-12°)	**September**	53-70° (12-21°)
April	43-60° (6-16°)	**October**	46-60° (8-16°)
May	49-68° (10-20°)	**November**	40-50° (5-10°)
June	55-73° (13-23°)	**December**	36-44° (2-7°)

Subject Index

Street Index

Paris Reflections
Your Thoughts on Your Visit to Paris